IT SAVVY

IT SAVVY

What Top Executives Must Know
to Go from Pain to Gain

PETER WEILL
JEANNE W. ROSS

HARVARD BUSINESS PRESS
BOSTON, MASSACHUSETTS

Printed in the United States of America
13 12 11 10   5 4 3 2

Library of Congress Cataloging-in-Publication Data

Weill, Peter.
    IT savvy : what non-IT executives should know to make IT pay off /
Peter Weill, Jeanne W. Ross.
        p. cm.
    ISBN 978-1-4221-8101-0 (hbk. : alk. paper)
    1.   Information technology—management.   I. Ross, Jeanne W. II. Title.
    HD30.2.W4496 2009
    004.068'4—dc22

                                                                2009005480

The paper used in this publication meets the requirements of the
American National Standard for Permanence of Paper for Publications
and Documents in Libraries and Archives Z39.48-1992.

CONTENTS

PREFACE AND
ACKNOWLEDGMENTS

As we write this preface, the business world is experiencing what looks like one of the most far-reaching financial crises in living memory. Banks, car-manufacturing companies, government agencies, nations, states, retirement funds, and overall confidence have all taken a pounding. One of our favorite management theorists is Niccolò Machiavelli (circa 1530). Machiavelli would have reminded us that you should never, never, never waste a perfectly good crisis.

As we work through this financial crisis, businesses will need to rethink how they operate. No longer will it suffice for firms to go through periods of spending for growth and then periods of rationalizing cost to increase margins. Today's global business environment and investment community demands simultaneous profit and growth. Achieving consistently profitable growth will mean managing to achieve rationalization and business agility simultaneously. This will require changing the way firms operate. Perhaps the crisis has an upside. People and organizations will be much more willing than usual to make the necessary and far-reaching changes that are usually very difficult. Machiavelli put it well: "There is nothing more difficult to take in hand, more perilous to conduct or more uncertain in its success than to take the lead in the introduction of a new order of things."[1] This book is about making those changes and creating a new order of things in your firm—a new order that is digital.

Now is the time for bold leaders to prepare their organizations for the next couple of decades. We think one of the biggest opportunities and challenges for you will be the digitization of business. Every interaction between a customer and a business, between a business and another business, between employees in a business, and between a government and a business will become more and more digital. Information technology (IT) spending will continue to increase in virtually every enterprise. Business processes—everything from order-to-cash, search-to-hire, or idea-to-launch—will become increasingly digital. The information that these digital processes produce will allow firms such as 7-Eleven Japan to continue being one of the most profitable retailers by having a real-time picture of what is selling across its more than twelve thousand stores. 7-Eleven Japan, no longer a traditional retailer, effectively brokers this information to its business partners—for a fee—across its network of franchised stores, distribution centers, manufacturers, and logistics providers. 7-Eleven Japan is one of the most IT-savvy companies around. It thrives in the digital economy.

A digital economy enables a business process to run flawlessly, twenty-four hours a day. Information is pervasive and sometimes overwhelming. Markets are electronic, and matching buyers and sellers is easy. Search is universal and fast. Many new products can be tested online and scaled quickly if successful. There are cybercrime and privacy issues, however, as well as the risk of system failures temporarily shutting down businesses. A digital economy therefore means we need a fundamentally different approach—and IT-savvy firms are leading the way.

Rather than identify the business need and build or acquire a system to meet that need, IT-savvy firms take a different approach. IT-savvy firms decide how they want to operate and proceed to build a digitized platform of business processes, IT systems, and data to execute on their operating strategy. These platforms not only utilize IT capability to repeatedly execute business process, but also provide the information to identify where future profitable growth will come from. Then, with marginal investment, these firms create the new products and services that are faster to market because they reuse the platform. Best of all, IT savvy pays off. IT-savvy firms are 20 percent more profitable than their competitors. This book is about what it means to be an IT-savvy leader and firm, why it's important to be IT savvy, and how to become more IT savvy.

We were motivated to write this book on a cold and wintry December day in Boston. We had just finished teaching in the MIT Sloan School of Management's "IT for the Non-IT Executive" program. This program—which runs three times a year—brings together eighty to one hundred senior executives at MIT to talk about how to get more business value from IT. We, along with our MIT Center for Information Systems Research (CISR) colleagues George Westerman and Chuck

Gibson, have been lucky enough to teach in this program since 2000. We usually commence the program by asking the executives to turn to a neighbor and describe what's wrong with IT in their firm. The conversations begin quietly, but soon there is an almighty din in the room as participants passionately explain their frustrations. It's a defining moment in the program when, several sessions later, we offer an explanation: perhaps you get the IT you deserve. If you change strategies often, or don't clarify how you want to operate the firm, or abdicate IT decisions and move rapidly from one project idea to the next, how can any organization excel in using IT? At best the IT unit will always be reactive and will never be able to get out in front of your organization's strategic needs.

This book is a summary of the lessons learned over the course of more than twenty years of research into what it takes to be IT savvy and how to get maximum value from IT. For the last ten years we have been fortunate to collaborate on much of that research and work with many great executives while at the MIT Sloan School of Management's Center for Information Systems Research. The book is a testimony to those senior executives with whom we have worked in MIT Sloan's executive programs, our research sites, and our facilitation work. Now we want to share what we have learned with all executives for debate and discussion.

WHO SHOULD READ THIS BOOK

This book is written for all executives who know, deep down, that IT is critical to their business and would like to learn how top performers manage IT. Based on field research in hundreds of firms, we have aimed to boil down to its essence what you need to do to make IT a strategic asset rather than a liability. We discuss the business and IT decisions with enough detail to guide implementation. The language, style, data, examples, and lessons are about business issues that rely on technology.

We encourage all managers to read this book and discuss how IT savvy they are today and where they would like to be in three years. More important, we encourage you to ask yourself, "What do I need to do differently? What are the practices we use today that have made us less IT savvy and gotten us into trouble?" For simplicity of language we adopted the word *firm* in this book. However, our comments relate equally to all organizations, whether they are large or small, for profit, not for profit, or government. Our intention is to capture the imagination and challenge the assumptions of managers in all industries as they lead their firms in an increasingly digital age.

THE RESEARCH

The insights in the book come from a series of research projects at MIT CISR on how top-performing firms generate superior business value from IT. We studied more than 1,800 companies in more than sixty countries during the period from 2000 to 2009. The main studies were as follows:

- *Business process management (2008):* Jeanne Ross conducted interviews with executives at forty firms about the development of their business process platforms and completed case studies at Pacific Life, Swiss Reinsurance, Campbell Soup, and PepsiAmericas.

- *MIT CISR survey of the CIOs and IT finance person in the same firms (2007–2008):* We administered a two-part survey to 1,508 firms in sixty countries, in partnership with Dr. Howard Rubin. One part of the survey was completed by the CIO and studied enterprise architecture, IT governance performance and mechanisms, CIO time allocations, and IT innovation. The second part of the survey was completed by an IT financial person and examined IT spending and investment decisions and technology practices. We also analyzed firm financial performance.

- *IT portfolio and IT savvy (2000–2008):* Peter Weill, Sinan Aral, and Stephanie Woerner studied IT portfolios and the impact on firm performance using several data sets. IT savvy was measured in two different ways and the impact assessed with a variety of analysis techniques, including several types of regression controlling for industry, size, and other important effects.

- *MIT SeeIT surveys of IT finances (2005 and 2006):* We surveyed the "IT financial person" in 626 firms in 2005 and 2006, in conjunction with Dr. Howard Rubin, in order to understand the relationships among IT investment, practices, and firm performance; this research was part of the MIT SeeIT Project, funded by the U.S. National Science Foundation (grant number IIS-0085725). We studied IT investment decisions, outsourcing practices, and drivers of company growth and agility. We also measured governance and firm financial performance, and the effectiveness of a number of organizational and governance practices.

- *Business process digitization (BPO) (2006–2008):* Peter Weill, Nils Fonstad (INSEAD), and Mani Subramani (University of Minnesota) studied twenty-four BPO relationships, collected data from 217 firms, and interviewed dozens of clients and service providers from a variety of industries based in different parts of the world. The study involved several trips to India and visits to firms including the following: Infosys, Jumpstart, MindTree, RelQ, Satyam, Setu, Sierra Atlantic, Syntel, TCS, Wipro, Wipro Global Radiology Services, Bally, Cisco, Honeywell, Microsoft, Rallis, one anonymous hardware systems company, State Street Corporation, and Textron, plus U.S. and U.K. clients of Indian service companies (five financial services and three manufacturing companies).

- *Global governance of IT (2006–2008) (focused on Asia):* Peter Weill, Christina Soh, and S. K. Siew (Nanyang Technological University) conducted multiple interviews to understand how large firms manage IT in Asia and globally. Firms included Procter & Gamble, Intel, Merrill Lynch, and Microsoft.

- *Future of the CIO (2007 and 2008):* Peter Weill and Stephanie Woerner conducted research on effective use of CIO time allocation:

  - Survey of 228 CIOs in twenty-six countries

  - Survey of 154 senior non-IT executives on how CIOs should spend their time

  - Interviews of a dozen CIOs in companies ranging in size from $1.5 billion to $70 billion

  - Discussions with Shawn Banerji, managing director, Russell Reynolds Associates

  - Interviews with five senior executive-level officers on how they want their CIOs to spend their time

- *Business agility (2005–2006):* Jeanne Ross and Cynthia Beath conducted interviews with twenty-three IT and business executives and did surveys with sixty firms to identify types and sources of agility and completed a case study at Southwest Airlines.

- *Outsourcing and enterprise architecture (2004–2005):* Case studies of architectural implications of outsourcing at eight firms by Jeanne Ross, Cynthia Beath, Jeff Sampler, and Nils Fonstad. We studied the relationship between the role of enterprise architecture in outsourcing decisions and the outcomes. The companies were Campbell, Carlson Companies, Dow Chemical Company, eFunds, JM Family, Tecnovate, and two others.

- *IT engagement models (2004–2006):* Case studies of Toyota Motor Marketing Europe, BT, ING DIRECT, and fifteen others by David Robertson and Nils Fonstad to explore the key issues regarding establishing effective engagement models.

- *New infrastructure capabilities, enterprise resource planning systems, and e-business initiatives (1995–2005):* Case studies of eighteen firms' IT implementations by Jeanne Ross, Mike Vitale, and Peter Weill. The cases focused on transformations leading to—and in some cases driven by—new IT capabilities. Companies included Australia Post, Brady Corporation, Chase Manhattan, Dow Corning, GTECH, JC Penney, Johnson & Johnson, Manheim, MetLife, Schneider, Texas Instruments, Travelers, USAA, the Washington, D.C. government, and four others.

- *Enterprise architecture outcomes (2004):* Surveys of 103 firms to assess architecture outcomes by Jeanne Ross and Nils Fonstad. We examined IT investments, architecture management practices, architecture maturity, and IT and business outcomes.

- *Business process outsourcing (2004):* Surveys of eighty firms' IT and business process outsourcing initiatives by Jeanne Ross and Cynthia Beath in conjunction with Lorraine Cosgrove at *CIO Magazine*. We examined the services outsourced, the characteristics of those services, the vendor-client relationship, architecture implications, and outcomes.

- *IT and business strategy (2001–2002):* Case studies at eight companies on the relationship between IT and business strategy by Jeanne Ross and Peter Weill. We studied how companies developed IT capabilities in response to business strategy. We also looked at how IT units were developing and managing enterprise architecture. Companies included Air Products, Citibank Asia, Delta Air Lines, DuPont, Merrill Lynch, Nestlé USA, Toyota USA, and UPS.

- *Enterprise architecture (2002):* Case studies on enterprise architecture at sixteen companies in the United States and Europe by Jeanne Ross, David Robertson, George Westerman, and Nils Fonstad. We studied how IT architecture enabled or constrained business initiatives. Cases were based on interviews with the CIO, IT architect, two project heads, and others at Akzo Nobel, BIC Graphic Europe, BT, Campbell Soup, Canon Europe, Carlson Companies, ING DIRECT, Marriott, Novartis, Panalpina, Partners Healthcare, Pfizer, Secheron, Swisscom Mobile, Tetra Pak, and Toyota Motor Marketing Europe.

- *IT governance (2001–2008):* Study on effective IT governance by Peter Weill with many colleagues during the period from 2001 to 2009. We studied over three hundred enterprises in more than thirty countries, including over twenty-five case studies. We studied how enterprises made five key IT decisions, including IT investment and prioritization. We also measured governance and financial performance and what practices worked best.

WHO WE WOULD LIKE TO THANK

We gratefully acknowledge the support of MIT CISR's patrons—Boston Consulting Group, BT Group, Diamond Management & Technology Consultants, Gartner, IBM, Microsoft, and Tata Consultancy Services—and sponsors (as of January 1, 2009): Aetna, Allstate Insurance, ANZ Banking Group (Australia), AstraZeneca Pharmaceuticals, Banco Itaú (Brazil), Banco Real (Brazil), BP, Campbell Soup, Canadian Imperial Bank of Commerce, CareFirst BlueCross BlueShield, Caterpillar, Celanese, Chevron, CHRISTUS Health, Chubb & Son, Commonwealth Bank of Australia, Credit Suisse (Switzerland), Det Norske Veritas (Norway), DHL Global Management (Germany), Direct Energy, Empresa Brasileira de Aeronautica (Brazil), EMC, ExxonMobil Global Services, Fidelity Investments, Guardian Life Insurance Company of America, Hartford Life, HBOS Australia, ING Groep (Netherlands), Intel, International Finance, Johnson & Johnson, Liberty Mutual Group, Marathon Oil, Mars, Merrill Lynch & Co., MetLife, Mohegan Sun, NASA, Nissan North America, Nomura Research Institute (Japan), Parsons Brinckerhoff, PepsiAmericas, PepsiCo International, Pfizer, PNC Global Investment Servicing, Procter & Gamble, Quest Diagnostics, Raytheon, Renault (France), Standard & Poor's, State Street Corporation, Sunoco, TD Bank, Time Warner Cable, Trinity Health, TRW

Automotive, Unibanco (Brazil), VF Corporation, Wal-Mart, and World Bank.

These enterprises not only inform and fund our research, but also probe our assumptions, test our ideas, debate our findings, and implement and improve our work. We could not do this work without them, and we are grateful they are part of the MIT CISR community.

During research and writing, we have had the opportunity to work with many extraordinary managers and academic colleagues who have influenced our thinking and reinforced our passions. First, we would like to acknowledge the managers who shared their insights and, in many cases, provided examples for the book. These managers included Yuka Ozaki, Toshifumi Suzuki, and Makoto Usui at 7-Eleven Japan; Al-Noor Ramji and J. P. Rangaswami at BT; Michael Moeller, Joe Spagnoletti, and Doreen Wright at Campbell Soup; Dave Keppler and Frank Luijckx at The Dow Chemical Company; Frank Wander of Guardian Life Insurance; Martin Vonk at ING DIRECT and Michael Vincent at ING; Martin Curley and Malvina Nisman at Intel; Michael Harte, Mark Potter, Mark Reed, Tim Whiteley, and all the senior IT and non-IT executives we worked with at CBA; Kumud Kalia at Direct Energy; Karl Wachs at Celanese; Jonathan White at Pfizer; Kristine Goodwin, Tom Lydon, and Rebecca Rhoads at Raytheon; Ken Johnsen, John Kreul, and Irina Raff at PepsiAmericas; Joe Antonellis, James Brunner, Robert Kaplan, Chris Perretta, David Saul, and Wendy Watson at State Street Corporation; Tony Scott and Emilio Umeoka at Microsoft; Pat Hewlett and her colleagues at ExxonMobil; Michael Brook and Ken Cooke at PricewaterhouseCoopers; Dave Barnes, Mike Eskew, Ken Lacy, and Jim Medeiros at UPS; Guido Kehl, Markus Schmid, Sylvia Steinmann, and Yury Zaytsev at Swiss Re; Rosalee Hermens at Timberland; Roland Paanakker at Nike; Richard Hoynes at Tyco; Brad Peterson at eBay; Julio Gomes, Pedro Moreira Salles, and their colleagues at Unibanco; Carlos Amesquita, Filippo Passerini, and Robert Scott at Procter & Gamble; Tom Nealon at JC Penney; Charlie Feld at EDS; Ken LeBlanc and Mark Quigley at EMC; Meg McCarthy and Ron Williams at Aetna; and Bob Jordan and Jan Marshall at Southwest Airlines.

We want to gratefully acknowledge all the managers who participated in case study interviews and those who took the time to answer our survey questions, add their own insights, and probe our assumptions. We are grateful to all of you for making this book possible.

Colleagues at other universities who contributed to the research in this book include Professor Sinan Aral at New York University, Professor Cynthia Beath at the University of Texas–Austin, Professor Mani Subramani at the Carlson School at the University of Minnesota, Professors Christina Soh and S. K. Siew at Nanyang Technological University in Singapore, and Dr. Nils Fonstad at INSEAD in France (formerly at MIT CISR). We want to especially thank Dr. Stephanie Woerner, research scientist at MIT CISR, who participated in much of this research.

Thanks to Koki Yodokawa and Kei Nagayama at Nomura Research Institute in Japan, who helped us understand why 7-Eleven Japan is so successful. We also want to thank the many people who provided important input and feedback to the research in this book, including John Sviokla and Chris Curran at Diamond Management & Technology Consultants; Mark McDonald at Gartner; Ananth Krishnan and Vipul Shah at TCS; Mark Ernest and Brian Barnier at IBM; and Samm DiStasio, Donald Koscheka, and Shafeen Charania at Microsoft. A big thank you to the many executives who made comments during our presentations or came up afterward to share their insights and debate the issues—we thrive on your passion.

We also want to acknowledge Juan Ayala of Microsoft for his insightful discussions drawing on his experience of helping companies worldwide improve their business value from IT.

In addition to anonymous reviewers, three colleagues read the entire manuscript and provided not only valuable comments but also much-appreciated enthusiasm and debate: Dr. Chuck Gibson at MIT CISR, Stuart Scantlebury of BCG, and Gail Pemberton-Burke at Korn Ferry. Thank you for your input—you will see your comments reflected in this final version.

We wish to thank Francisco González-Meza Hoffmann, Donna Pitteri, Susie Lee, Richard Woodham, Jason Chapman, Arthur Villa, Jamie Buckley, and Emmett Johnson, all researchers at MIT CISR, who helped conduct research used in this book. Individually and together as a team they added precision, professionalism, collegiality, and insight.

Our MIT CISR colleagues David Fitzgerald III, Chris Foglia, and Tea Huot managed the book production process with enthusiasm and professionalism. They devised the chapter template, produced the figures, enforced version control, tracked down citations, checked for contradictions, proofread, created innovations in collaboration tools, and almost kept us on schedule. We benefited from all their hard work, encouragement, and world-class can-do attitudes.

The writing of this book, as well as our ongoing research efforts, would not be possible without the support of our colleagues at MIT CISR and the Sloan School of Management. Chris Foglia brings new energy and great aptitude to her role as MIT CISR associate director every day. She has proven that there is no strategic, technical, financial, artistic, or organizational issue at MIT CISR that she cannot address. Tea Huot has brought to MIT CISR a calm confidence, a great eye, a can-do attitude, and extraordinary organizational skills. We are lucky to have him on our team. We also welcome Erika Larson to MIT CISR and the panache she brings to the group. To Anita Horn of Sloan IT, we say a huge thank you for keeping us up and humming. And we are indebted to our research colleagues: Nils Fonstad, Chuck Gibson, Wanda Orlikowski, Jack Rockart, George Westerman, Stephanie Woerner, and visiting scholar Lynne Markus. We have benefited enormously from their warmth, encouragement, insights, and camaraderie, and from their being part of the MIT CISR family.

MIT CISR is a research center in the Sloan School of Management. We are very proud and privileged to work in such a rich and exciting research environment. We have benefited from the support and encouragement of Deans David Schmittlein, Steven Eppinger, JoAnne Yates, and Rob Freund, as well as former Area Head professor Wanda Orlikowski and IT Group Head professor Thomas Malone.

We are delighted to again work with the incredible Kirsten Sandberg at Harvard Business Press. Kirsten, as our editor on this and four previous books, has a wonderful understanding of when to nudge, when to critique, and when to support. Kirsten continually adds value, and we are most grateful to her and her colleagues at HBS Press.

This book is the most recent of many wonderful collaborations between the two of us. We share the same values about what is important to executives and how research can help. But we come at the problem from two different research perspectives, and it's the product of these two perspectives that generates the richness and insights we hope you find in this book. Bringing those two perspectives together involves lots of heartfelt debates, often conducted at breakneck speed and with great passion. There is nothing quite so challenging and ultimately satisfying as being absolutely certain you are right—until you are convinced by the other person that there is another, and better, answer. We hope our collaboration continues well into our dotage.

A Personal Note from Peter

I would like to dedicate this book to the newest member of the small but global Weill family—Liam Hugo Weill, who joined us in December 2008. LHW and his contemporaries represent the future, and I hope that they will cherish the good we leave them and rectify what we got wrong.

I would like to thank my colleagues at MIT. A manager in Singapore recently asked me how I liked working at MIT. Without pausing, I found myself saying, "I moved to MIT about ten years ago, and academically I have reached Nirvana." I feel honored and fortunate to be part of the MIT community and to work every day at the MIT Sloan School of Management's Center for Information Systems Research. I now have a new global role, which allows me to work with executives all over the world to better understand and communicate how to get maximum business value from IT. I feel privileged.

My interest in the topic of gaining business value from IT began during my first job. I was assistant to the manufacturing director of an international consumer products company that spent freely on IT. I fondly remember my last task every Friday night: I had to carry a pack of large magnetic tapes by hand the mile or so from the glasshouse computer center in the production facility to the glasshouse computer center in the accounting department. The tapes contained the week's production figures for entry into the accounting system. The company was relatively IT savvy for its time. But I always felt we didn't know enough about how to maximize value. The story was mostly the same when I talked to executives in other enterprises. We should have done better—and we got nowhere close to the success a few firms achieved. How did they do it? I have spent my whole career so far trying to answer that question. This book is, in part, our answer to that question.

I would like to thank my wife, Dr. Margi Olson, who is my partner in life, best friend, collaborator, and ardent critic. As we move through life together I realize every day how fortunate I am in being with you. Somehow you manage to be, all at once, supportive, loving, insightful, generous, and one of the fiercest wielders of the red pen I know. Thanks for always being ready to debate—over and over—why firms act as they do and not the way we think they should. Thanks also for being such an insightful and lifelong student of organizations.

To my mother, Hilde Weill, thanks for your love, generous spirit, good genes, and great values. To my Aussie family Weill—Stephen, Lois, David, and Simon—thanks for all your love and support, and it's great to spend some more time with you. To my U.S. family Weill—Geoffrey, Noa, Benjamin, Zoe, and now Liam; and my Mumbai family Weill—Ilan, Sharon, Sean, Ashley, and Tommy. Thanks for helping me understand it better and feel part of family Weill. And to my other U.S. family—Jed, Maria, Katie O, and Quinn—I love you guys. Finally to Tim Schlager of Two Good—thanks for keeping my body moving despite the challenges.

A Personal Note from Jeanne

We are finishing this book as my husband Dan and I close out one of the most chaotic of our thirty-one years together. Thank you, Dan, for your love and support, and for moving back to Boston. Every day on my walk to work I marvel at how lucky I am. You are the biggest part of my good fortune.

I want to thank Adam, Julie, and Steffie for all the joy you bring to our lives. We treasure our time with you and love the vicarious adventures you've given us.

To my parents, Russ and Mary Wenzel, thanks for your love, support, and encouragement. You give so much and ask for so little. And to my siblings, Pat and Jim, Jo, Barb and Mark, Russ and Diane, and Dave and Jill, thanks for the pure pleasure of time spent with family. It's never enough.

And to Cindy and Stuart Lazarus, thanks for giving birth to chapter 1 at your lovely place on Seabrook Island. You know how to be fun even when your guests aren't so much. And thanks for your comments, Stuart—they got us going.

Finally, thanks to our Columbus friends, who remain so dear, and our Acton friends, who have welcomed us back. We count you among our most cherished blessings.

Transforming IT from Strategic Liability to Strategic Asset

In 2002, when Ron Williams became president of the U.S. health care services giant Aetna, the company had just reported an annual loss of $280 million and was on the brink of failure.[1] In 2007, just five years later, Aetna posted net income of $1.8 billion and was named by *Fortune* magazine the United States' most admired company in health care. To what does Williams, now CEO and chairman, attribute the company's turnaround? An intense focus on customers and employees, a companywide embrace of "back to basics" values, and the development and use of a dynamic information technology (IT) platform.[2]

Williams joined Aetna in 2000 as head of business operations. Early on, he initiated a project to develop an executive management information system (EMIS). Implemented within five months, Aetna's early EMIS provided point-and-click access and drill-down capability on the income statements of both the enterprise and its divisions. Williams used the available data as the basis for executive decisions. In addition, he and then-CEO John Rowe made clear that they expected business executives to use data to drive better business performance. Firmwide delivery of transparent and consistent performance data gave them an opportunity, as Williams described it, to "train the company how to think about problems. It gives you the context for making choices."

Armed with useful data, Aetna's senior managers started making what one observer called "surgical decisions" on prices in their proposals to institutional customers. Turning attention to profitability rather than revenues, Aetna deliberately set prices that led to a decrease in memberships for a couple of years. Over time, the EMIS helped management better define and address the company's market segments. Soon, both revenues and profits were growing. In 2007, Aetna reported revenues of $27.6 billion, a 35 percent increase over three years.

The EMIS was just the first step in using IT to make Aetna's people smarter and more productive. Subsequent enhancements have provided systems enabling the firm to refocus business processes on the needs of customers. For example,

Aetna started providing customers online access to medical advice and information about their accounts and history. These efforts have transformed Aetna into a highly respected and profitable health care company.

Aetna is unusual. Many leaders we talk with are frustrated because they don't see significant benefits from IT despite millions of dollars of IT investments. They struggle to meet basic requirements for doing business in a global economy. Often, they can't:

- Respond to new customer opportunities in a timely manner

- Present a single face to global customers

- Reproduce business successes in a new market

- Integrate new acquisitions quickly

- Ensure that local decision makers simultaneously do what's best for customers and the firm

In short, they can't operate how they want to operate. And frankly, if IT isn't helping you operate how you want—and need—to operate, you are wasting money. There is no chance that your IT investments will lead to strategic benefits.

Aetna is IT savvy. The company consistently uses IT to inform management decisions and enhance products and services. Being IT savvy makes IT a strategic asset. In a global, digital economy, if IT is not a strategic asset, it's a strategic liability. Ask yourself: in the twenty-first century, can you afford to have a liability like that?

WHAT IS IT SAVVY (AND HOW DO WE GET SOME)?

IT savvy is a characteristic of firms and their managers reflected in the ability to use IT to consistently elevate firm performance. Like *savoir faire*, IT savvy looks effortless from the outside. But IT-savvy firms distinguish themselves from others by building and using a platform of digitized processes.

A *digitized platform* is an integrated set of electronic business processes and the technologies, applications, and data supporting those processes. Not all business processes are digitized—many require human intervention. And not all digitized processes are part of a platform—the platform integrates a set of related processes and transactions.

At some firms, the digitized platform is anchored in a major piece of purchased software such as an enterprise resource planning system or a customer relationship management system.[3] At other firms, the IT unit has built an enterprise data and technology platform for operation decisions. People provide input to a digitized platform and use the output, but people are not part of the platform itself. The purpose of a digitized process platform is to disengage people from processes that are better performed by machines. The platform "wires" reliable, predictable, low-cost core business transactions into the firm.

At Aetna, the digitized process platform encompasses the daily servicing of customer needs, ranging from opening an account to settling a claim. Aetna has built a solid technology base and layered it with reliable, predictable business processes for daily transactions. The reliability and predictability of daily transactions is only the beginning, however. Aetna, like all IT-savvy firms, uses the data generated from its core transactions to empower decision makers. IT-savvy firms make a habit of executing disciplined core processes and then applying the resulting data from those processes to both operational and strategic decision-making tasks.

IT-savvy firms are not necessarily high-tech firms. In our research we have encountered only a small number of IT-savvy firms. Without exception, these firms use IT to "wire in" core transactions, and they use the data from their core transactions to inform decision making. Our list of IT-savvy firms includes highly successful new-age e-businesses such as Amazon, eBay, and Google. But long-established brick-and-mortar firms can also become IT savvy. Take, for example, 7-Eleven Japan, United Parcel Service, and Procter & Gamble.

- *7-Eleven Japan (SEJ):* SEJ uses IT to empower its people—all its people—with information. Often, the most profitable retailer in Japan, SEJ provides standard systems across the firm's 12,034 stores and 1,100 vendor, manufacturer, and distributor locations.[4] These systems support ordering, inventory management, production management, and logistics. Every salesclerk at 7-Eleven Japan has access to a handheld device for ordering stock. A constant flow of graphical data, showing recent sales, weather conditions, and product range information, informs clerks at SEJ stores. These salesclerks, both full-time and part-time, make hypotheses, such as how many Bento boxes (on warm days) or hot noodles (on cold days) to order. In a day or two, they receive feedback on the business results of their hypotheses. This feedback cycle constantly hones SEJ's inventory and revenue management decisions, leading to both operational excellence and product innovation. Because of SEJ's combination of real-time information, fast feedback, empowered local decision making, and standardized business processes, a stunning 70 percent of SEJ's products are new each year in each store.

- *United Parcel Service (UPS):* Focused initially on matching Federal Express's capability to track packages, the world's largest package delivery company now uses IT to optimize operations and enhance profitability.[5] UPS equips its drivers with a DIAD (delivery information acquisition device), which captures a customer signature and uploads data on each delivery to the company's package information database. UPS analyzes this data to better understand the profitability of individual customers and packages, which leads to improved routing and pricing decisions. UPS has an industrial engineering culture—internal experts regularly study UPS's operations to identify opportunities for increased efficiencies. UPS then builds systems to support end-to-end processes. In addition, partnerships with software vendors such as SAP and Oracle allow UPS customers to access UPS package information electronically, thereby making not only UPS, but also UPS's customers, more efficient. This combination of powerful package data, disciplined operations, and customer-oriented electronic services has helped UPS grow quickly and profitably in the United States and internationally.

- *Procter & Gamble (P&G):* P&G uses IT to focus management attention on the firm's distinctive marketing and distribution competencies. To accomplish that feat, P&G created Global Business Services (GBS), a shared services organization, to provide many of the firm's common, repetitive, non-unique services. GBS blends business processes and IT under the CIO to provide a base of seventy shared services for the firm's 250 marketing units. Services range from core technology services, such as e-mail and telecommunications, to major business support services, such as customer relationship management systems and competitive intelligence. GBS delivers reliable, cost-effective services so that brand managers can focus on what makes P&G distinctive—brand management. This arrangement allows P&G to realize both global economies of scale and reduced time to market for new products and services. The efficiencies GBS provides have helped P&G increase its net earnings margin from 12 percent in 2004 to 14.5 percent in 2008.[6]

It can be difficult to distinguish these three firms' IT savvy from their outstanding business management. Indeed, a characteristic of IT-savvy firms is that IT is at the heart of highly effective management. IT is the platform and scaffolding for a structure that delivers world-class operations and strategically focused management decision making. None of the executives in these firms will tell you that IT is all they need to be successful. But, then again, IT is never an afterthought at these firms. Rather, IT forms the basis for each firm's competitive capabilities.

Perhaps this sounds fine for companies like UPS and P&G, but your company has other formulas for achieving distinctive competitive advantage. Good luck! That attitude should guarantee that as the world's global business economy increasingly depends on timely information, predictable and cost-effective operations, and rapidly implemented strategic experiments, your firm won't be in the game. If you want to succeed in the global digital economy, you need IT to serve as the platform for your business operations. Yes, in many cases you've already built the house your firm lives in, and now we're telling you that you need to build a foundation under that house. It won't be easy.

IT-savvy firms do not suddenly "strike it IT rich." Instead, they build knowledge and business process capabilities over time. They convert their operational knowledge and digitized processes into an ever-growing digitized platform. Aetna, 7-Eleven Japan, UPS, and P&G, among others, offer proof that it's possible to transform an established firm into an IT-savvy firm.

At IT-savvy firms, IT is a strategic asset including one or more digitized platforms. A small but growing number of firms have developed their unique digitized platform. Other firms have started to build platforms, but they haven't yet learned how to drive value from them. Their platforms are stagnating—or worse, disintegrating. For these firms—and the many that have not, as yet, defined a platform—IT is a strategic liability.

HOW IT BECOMES A LIABILITY

A number of years ago, the highly respected CEO of a process manufacturer said to us: "I've been reading [up]on IT, but I'm terrified. It's the one area where I don't feel competent. I sense that we're not getting good value for our money."

This CEO's sentiments are not unusual. Senior executives naturally take charge of their people, their budgets, and their strategies, but they often look to hand off their IT responsibilities to someone else. IT may be a ubiquitous business tool, but it can bring otherwise competent managers to their knees.

Senior management's lack of confidence is dangerous, because it usually results in leaders abdicating responsibility for IT in the company. If senior managers do not accept accountability for IT, the company will inevitably throw its IT dollars at a myriad of tactical initiatives with no significant impact on organizational capabilities.

Does this pattern sound familiar?

1. A line business manager prepares a compelling business case for a new product or service.

2. After some hearty debate (or perhaps a quick rubber stamp), management allocates resources

and establishes a schedule and budget for implementation of the new system.

3. Business managers explain the concept to IT managers and provide some requirements.

4. IT people work hard to clarify the requirements and deliver the system on time and within budget.

5. In response to constantly changing business demands and demonstrations of system prototypes, business managers adjust the requirements for the new system.

6. IT people start working nights and weekends to address changes and meet the schedule (having abandoned the budget).

7. The system is delivered late with less than intended functionality. Nonetheless, the new product or service it supports succeeds in the marketplace.

8. The new system is added to the firm's inventory of isolated systems solutions, which the IT unit patches together and manages very carefully to make sure nothing breaks.

This piecemeal approach to IT results in some valuable IT-based products and services, but it also requires the IT unit to spend more and more time tying together systems and data that were designed independently. Management finds that it takes longer and longer to test new systems and integrate them with existing systems. The patchwork of systems makes the firm increasingly vulnerable to systems outages, and the firm finds it increasingly difficult to respond to changing business conditions.

Ultimately, the systems environment starts to look like figure 1-1, a set of isolated systems wired together to meet the next immediate need. These systems are as inelegantly bound together as cold spaghetti. They behave a lot like cold spaghetti, too. Any attempt to change or extract one system risks breaking another. As a result, the average firm spends 71 percent of its IT budget operating and maintaining these systems—funds that are then not available to introduce new products or services.

FIGURE 1-1

The typical systems landscape in a non-IT-savvy firm

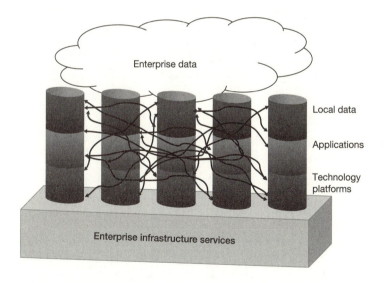

Source: © 2009 MIT Sloan Center for Information Systems Research. Used with permission.

Many firms spend as much as 80 percent of their IT budgets on running current systems, whereas some IT-savvy firms spend as little as 50 percent, leaving them with relatively more money for new business initiatives.[7]

Figure 1-1 does not just reflect ineffective systems; it also shows the tangle of business processes that use these systems to deliver goods and services to customers. This is how work gets done in complex organizations. People work hard to somehow meet customer expectations by working around, or compensating for, the disjointed systems and processes that have grown up over time.

The fundamental limitation of this piecemeal approach to systems is that it can never result in a foundation for effective business processes—a digitized platform. Without such a platform, every customer-oriented business process is dependent on the instincts, judgment, and attention of the person completing it. No matter how great your people, they cannot compensate for undisciplined business processes. An undisciplined company competing against a firm with a well-oiled digitized platform will consistently come up short.

Reversing a firm's IT fortunes requires different thinking from the type that helped the firm create its messy legacy. But some of the most common fixes that senior managers apply to IT typically make their problems worse. Perhaps you've seen some of these approaches—at other firms of course!

- *Throw more money at IT problems.* This strategy suggests that a firm has plenty of money but not much time or discipline. Management is willing to throw resources at the problem but is not willing to force changes in behavior. In the end, this approach will lead to increased spending but not to increased benefits.

- *Drastically cut IT spending.* This strategy is a sensible approach to dealing with spending that isn't generating benefits. Stop the spending. We have seen firms benefit in the short term from this strategy, because the reduced spending forced a serious dialogue about the firm's priorities. Such focus can be valuable. But be aware that a sustained strategy of simply not spending on IT will eventually undermine the firm's ability to perform in the global, digitally connected economy.

- *Fire the CIO.* If the firm just needs someone to blame, management may be inclined to bring in a new face. As with any senior management position, it's possible that a firm has an ineffective CIO, but it's often the case that the rest of the management team hasn't embraced its responsibilities to define and implement effective business processes. Blaming the CIO may simply be one way for business leaders to abdicate accountability for IT.

- *Outsource the IT problem.* Outsourcing can be a valuable way of bringing in world-class talent, but effective outsourcing requires world-class management internally. Often, wholesale outsourcing is just another attempt to acquire effective IT without changing behavior in other parts of the firm. Invariably, if IT costs too much and its benefits are too little, the dysfunctional behaviors are as apparent in the business as in IT. IT costs and services are not likely to improve significantly with outsourcing until business people change their habits.

- *Yank out legacy systems and replace them with a huge vendor-developed integrated solution.* This approach has helped a number of companies tame their systems and processes. But many companies have made the mistake of thinking that a big package will solve their problems, when what's required is a major management change initiative. The package can support an enterprisewide business change initiative, but the system alone will do little to change a company's fortunes.

If your systems and processes are broken, you'll need to change how you think about IT and how you implement digitized processes. Most important, you'll need to lead the transformation to an IT-savvy company.

THREE OBSESSIONS OF THE IT-SAVVY FIRM

Firms striving to convert IT from a strategic liability to a strategic asset face some big challenges. They will be ripping out legacy systems and processes and then implementing new business processes and systems. This effort involves far more than IT work—it's a business transformation.

To succeed in this transformation, management must pursue three activities. First, senior executives have to fix what's broken in their management and use of IT. This means they have to introduce new ways of thinking about and funding IT. Second, IT and business leaders have to build a digitized platform. A digitized platform is rapidly becoming a prerequisite for the opportunity to compete in the digital economy. Third, business leaders must exploit their digitized platform for profitable growth. Putting in a digitized platform provides business opportunities, but firms are not equally successful in driving benefits from their platforms.

Becoming IT savvy often requires making these activities a management obsession. Otherwise, it's easy to fall back on old habits. Let us describe what these efforts look like.

Fixing What's Broken About IT

Figure 1-1 highlights the vulnerability of firms' systems and processes. Inevitably, behind the scenes of messy legacy systems and processes, we see a broken accountability framework and decision-making model. As long as you don't have buy-in to a clear, enterprisewide approach to how IT will support your strategy, you will continue to pile on spaghetti instead of building a digitized platform. IT-savvy firms have addressed their legacy problems by providing both a clear vision for how IT will support business operations and a well-understood funding model focused on delivering the vision.

For example, Aetna had, for many years, built each new system to support a single insurance product. As a result, Aetna entered the twenty-first century with multiple, redundant processes and systems and fragmented customer data. The company had multiple approaches for core activities such as opening an account, underwriting a policy, and paying a claim. Aetna's management structures and decision-making processes reinforced its piecemeal business processes. The result was that Aetna had no good way to provide a single view of a customer's account.

To improve its systems and processes, Aetna first had to think in terms of how it wanted to deliver goods and services to customers. In doing so, Aetna reorganized the business around its major customer segments, redefined its business processes in terms of customer requirements, and reengineered the IT project funding process to focus on enterprise initiatives rather than product silos. These were critical steps in preparing to build a digitized platform.

Building a Digitized Platform

Once you've changed your approach to IT, you're ready to build a digitized platform. This platform provides stable core operations even in turbulent business environments. It can't be built in a day, however, so you'll need to map out a path of increasingly powerful and connected systems and processes. Start by identifying what's *not* changing. The core business processes in your firm that are not changing define a reliable set of reusable IT-supported data and processes. The digitized platform standardizes and automates these processes, thereby increasing reliability, decreasing operational cost, and ensuring quality.[8] This digitized platform allows you to focus management attention on what *is* changing in your marketplace.

Aetna's platform development focused initially on the data that would allow integration of business processes to meet customer needs. The company defined five categories of operational data: claims, enrollment (or member), product, plan, and provider. Management established shared definitions for the shared data and reengineered some business processes to ensure data accuracy and access. After several years, building this platform remains a work in process, but Aetna has continuously improved the decision-making processes and operations that rely on this data. The five "books of record," as Aetna managers refer to their data, are the core of Aetna's digitized platform.

Exploiting the Platform for Profitable Growth

Fixing what's broken and building a platform are both demanding undertakings, but now comes the hard—and fun—part. Management must also lead organizational change and drive value from a new asset—the digitized platform. To cash in on your platform, you will be changing individual roles, organizational structures, and the organizational culture. This is a fundamental business change and, thus, a major leadership challenge.

At Aetna, Ron Williams emphasized the need for data-driven decision making and spearheaded the effort to put consistent, reliable data in managers' hands. He and John Rowe, his predecessor as CEO, also encouraged employees to leverage the firm's data to develop new products and services for customers. One such service, the Aetna Navigator, which provided online medical advice for individuals, won accolades for being the best of its kind.[9]

Aetna, like the other firms cited in this chapter, has, for years, been working obsessively on fixing what's broken, building a digitized platform, and driving value from IT. In large, established organizations, becoming IT savvy is always a multiyear effort requiring persistent management time and effort. Is it worth it? You bet it is. Our research has found that IT-savvy firms have 20 percent higher margins than their competitors.[10]

Making IT a strategic asset starts with strong leadership. But even good leaders may question their ability to incorporate the capabilities of IT into their strategic thinking. This book is intended first as motivation and then as a guide for becoming IT savvy. We break down the three obsessions into five steps and devote a chapter to each step.

Chapters 2 and 3 examine how firms fix what's broken. First, we discuss how managers develop a clear vision of the role of IT and how the firm will operate. Then we discuss IT funding models, because money is the common denominator in firms. It's important to spend a sensible amount on IT—not too much and not too little. But it's even more important to target IT investments on initiatives that matter. We'll describe how IT-savvy firms meet that test.

Chapters 4 and 5 describe the multiyear process of building a digitized platform. We explain the capabilities firms develop as they build their platforms. Then we review how firms allocate decision rights and accountabilities—in other words, how they govern—to ensure that the platform is built and used.

Chapter 6 describes the process of driving value from the platform by discussing how IT-savvy firms develop business agility and introduce business innovation. We argue that agility and innovation are different, but complementary, processes allowing IT-savvy firms to progressively generate greater benefits from IT.

Finally, chapter 7 offers some actions you should take today to increase the business value your firm gets from IT in both the near term and over time. We discuss the critical role of senior management in making IT a strategic asset.

We hope you will find this guide motivating and helpful in making your firm IT savvy and that you enjoy the results.

Defining Your Operating Model

Consider a professional sports team—a good team, but not championship caliber. What will it take to convert the team into a champion? First, you decide how you want to operate to reach your championship vision. How do we coordinate the players, coaches, scouts, general managers, marketing, fan base, and facilities? Until the team gets that right, there's no point worrying about who starts the next game, prices for tickets, or the hiring and training plan for players.

Developing an IT-savvy firm is a similar exercise. First, you have to define a vision. Then you can address how you will create an integrated platform of strategy, players, facilities, marketing, scouting, and training to profit and grow. Many firms have not yet addressed the question of how they want the firm to profit and grow, and how IT can help create their platform. In effect, they can't ever become a championship team.

Information technology does two things well: integration and standardization. Recognizing this, IT-savvy firms clarify what they are trying to do with IT by specifying what they want to integrate and standardize. In doing so, they are defining an operating model. The operating model states the objectives of a firm's digitized platform and establishes its basic requirements.

At many firms, IT is used to provide short-term solutions to immediate problems. Their approach to IT is broken. To fix what's broken, you have to start by defining your operating model.

SPECIFYING REQUIREMENTS FOR INTEGRATION AND STANDARDIZATION

CEMEX, the US$22 billion global building materials company, has an operating model that specifies highly standardized management practices across all its businesses. In the early 1990s, the CEO, Lorenzo Zambrano, established a vision for growth that involved rapid deployment of standard CEMEX management practices in a succession of acquisitions. CEMEX built "The CEMEX Way," a platform of technology, systems, and business processes that captured CEMEX's best practices in finance, human resources (HR), and supply chain management.[1] CEMEX then installed this platform in its successive acquisitions.

Driving the benefits of the firm's operating model, Zambrano has grown CEMEX from what was Mexico's second-largest cement company in 1990 into a powerhouse global materials company. For its largest acquisition, the July 2007 acquisition of Rinker Group Limited, CEMEX needed less than six months to start realizing over US$400 million in synergies.

UPS has also benefited from a clear operating model. UPS's vision, dating back to the late 1980s, was to provide globally integrated, highly standardized package delivery services. To help achieve that vision, management viewed its first package tracking application as more than just an immediate solution. Package tracking required global access to a package database. So UPS designed the only package database it ever intended to implement, as well as a global telecommunications network through which employees and customers could access it. UPS has leveraged its digitized platform to develop customer services that share information on both incoming and outgoing shipments. Its innovative uses of package data make package information as valuable to UPS as the package.[2]

The decision to standardize both processes and data provided the basic design for UPS's digitized platform. That platform created opportunities for increasingly valuable systems. Michael Eskew, former CEO of UPS, noted that business and IT leaders regularly proposed IT-based customer services that could be quickly implemented. He referred to these suggestions as "happy surprises."[3]

IT conversations that lead to new customer services may be happy surprises, but they certainly aren't accidents. The surprises take root in a digitized platform. That platform grows out of a clear vision—provided by senior management—of how the firm will operate.

If you want this kind of value from IT, you have to stop thinking of IT as a set of solutions and start thinking about integration and standardization. Integration provides data access across a business to enable end-to-end processes (e.g., order-to-cash, opening an account) or a single face to customers. Standardization reduces variation in business processes to increase quality, efficiency, and predictability in customer interactions and back office operations.

Your *operating model* is the targeted level of business process integration and business process standardization for how you want to deliver goods and services to customers. Your operating model establishes the design parameters for a digitized platform that can enable future business opportunities, just like the platforms at CEMEX and UPS.

FOUR IT-SAVVY COMPANIES, FOUR OPERATING MODELS

Firms define different integration and standardization requirements depending on their visions for how they can best profit and grow. Presented here are four examples of IT-savvy firms and their operating models. Their different operating models lead to very different digitized platforms. In the first example, you'll note that Procter & Gamble wants to maximize the benefits of having 250 smart and creative brand management units.

Management has built a platform of shared services that drives some enterprisewide synergies without limiting local autonomy.

Procter & Gamble: Shared Services Supporting Independent Businesses

Procter & Gamble is a 170-year-old consumer products goods company with worldwide revenues of more than $80 billion.[4] Procter & Gamble operates in 180 countries and territories marketing over 250 brands to more than five billion consumers. Approximately one-third of Procter & Gamble's sales—which are growing at double-digit rates—come from developing countries.

P&G is organized around three global business units: beauty and health (e.g., Wella, Pantene hair care, Crest toothpaste), household care (e.g., Folgers coffee, Dawn detergent), and Gillette (razors, Braun, Duracell batteries). Management values the innovativeness and customer responsiveness that autonomous business unit heads and brand managers contribute to the firm. But in the highly competitive consumer products goods industry, P&G also needs to pursue business efficiencies. To spearhead business efficiency, P&G has created Global Business Services (GBS), a shared services organization run by the CIO, Filipo Passerini.

As Passerini explains, GBS provides a platform for business growth by allowing P&G to quickly add a new brand or grow the brands it already has: "By blending business process and technology, we at GBS provide solutions to the rest of Procter & Gamble. We provide the building blocks for the marketing units to reduce their time to market globally."

GBS relies on sixty-five hundred Procter & Gamble people and vendor partners to deliver more than seventy services in two categories: employee services and solutions and business services and solutions (see table 2-1 for examples of services in both categories). A single catalogue lists the costs and service levels for each service and indicates which are mandatory and which are optional.

GBS was created in 1999, when some early technology and back office services formed the beginning of a digitized platform. GBS continues to create new services, adding new layers to its platform of standard services. GBS conceives the services, works the pricing, and markets the solutions. To encourage autonomous business managers to use shared solutions, GBS guarantees a 10 to 30 percent cost reduction to adopters of a shared service. In addition, GBS guarantees an annual glide-path reduction in unit price. Sophisticated IT financial management and governance ensure ongoing business value.

A digitized platform providing enterprise shared services creates synergies among autonomous businesses. Such a platform will not meet the needs of firms trying to maximize the accessibility of customer and product data. PepsiAmericas is an example of a firm building a digitized platform of accessible core data.

PepsiAmericas: Creating a Data Asset

PepsiAmericas, the world's second-largest manufacturer, seller, and distributor of PepsiCo beverages, was formed from a combination of three U.S. regional PepsiCo bottlers in 1999.[5] With 2007 sales of US$4.5 billion and an average of 10 percent growth per year, PepsiAmericas also does business in the

TABLE 2-1

Procter & Gamble's Global Business Services

EMPLOYEE SERVICES AND SOLUTIONS

Employee services	Pay, benefits, policies, career development, work plans
People management	Compensation planning, relocation, employee management tools
Facilities	Office moves, conveniences: banking, dining, fitness centers, mail, and documents
Computers and communications	PCs, e-mail, mobile phones, intranet, service support
Meetings	Rooms, technology and scheduling, audio and video conferencing, events
Travel	Booking, expense accounting, credit cards, group meetings

BUSINESS SERVICES AND SOLUTIONS

Purchases	Strategic sourcing, supplier relationship management, procurement service
Financial services and solutions	General ledger, affiliate accounting, product/fixed asset accounting, expense, sales/marketing accounting, purchases-to-payment (includes accounts payable), banking, financial reporting
Product innovation	Bioinformatics systems, product imaging and modeling systems
Supply network solutions	Demand planning systems, total order management, physical distance systems
Consumer solutions	Prime prospect research, CRM systems, advertising and media measurement
Customer solutions	Shopper intelligence, in-store action planning, trade fund management systems
Initiative management	Technical package and materials design, package artwork process, portfolio tracking and reporting
Business performance solutions	Decision cockpits, market mix modeling, competitive intelligence, ad hoc business analyses

Source: Procter & Gamble documentation.

Caribbean and central and eastern Europe. But 75 percent of the firm's revenues are generated in the United States, where 20,000-plus employees bottle and can beverages at 32 plants, stage them in 187 distribution facilities, and deliver them directly to stores and other customers using 7,200 vehicles.

For many years, soft drink bottling was a volume business with huge scale efficiencies. But the growing numbers of products, packaging options, and customer types means that truck drivers who formerly carried 35 to 40 unique products in their trucks now carry 200 to 300 products. As a result, bottling has changed from a scale business to one in which profitability depends on precise inventory management, accurate sales prediction, and careful revenue management. Accordingly, PepsiAmericas' operating model calls for tight coordination of information related to both customers and products.

To provide the needed information, PepsiAmericas has been building a centralized enterprise data repository and data warehouse. The data repository makes available real-time data on key items such as orders, production, inventory, and sales. PepsiAmericas took advantage of this data platform in 2007, when management transformed the firm's regional sales and delivery organization to a structure based on key customer segments and channels. Because of the data repository, the reorganization triggered very little IT work, but it supported more centralized pricing decisions.

COO Ken Keiser explains the strategic implications of the reorganization and the data platform that supports it:

> *[Pricing is now] done with a lot more historical data, both internal and external, like from Nielsen and IRI, and the IT*

systems play a big role in that. The pricing architecture, from a financial standpoint, is probably one of the most important things that we do. It's all about understanding volume, retail price, retailers' margin requirements, making trade-offs. And those are all affected by what you sell every day and what your promotional prices are . . . And if you can have all of your data in some centralized place, you can develop your ultimate revenue management strategy.

The reorganization to customer segments and channels was just one step in leveraging data to improve performance. The data repository has helped PepsiAmericas achieve top vendor awards from key customers such as Wal-Mart, Target, and Kroger. PepsiAmericas has also used the data to improve demand planning and forecasting accuracy to reduce stock-outs. Coupled with new warehousing technologies, PepsiAmericas' operational data is contributing to increased warehouse efficiency and loading accuracy.

Although data is the critical integrating mechanism—and thus the core of the digitized platform—for PepsiAmericas, an integrated data platform is not a recipe for success for every firm. ING DIRECT is building successful global operations on a set of standard products and business processes.

ING DIRECT: Creating a Platform of Standard Products and Processes

ING DIRECT, a subsidiary of the Dutch financial services giant ING, was founded in 1997 as a telephone bank in Canada.[6] One of the fastest-growing companies in history, ING DIRECT is a direct-to-customer operation offering core banking products to

21.5 million customers of nine country bank organizations in Europe, North America, Asia, and Australia via Internet, mail, or phone.

ING DIRECT is a personal bank and does not have global customers. Every individual doing business with ING DIRECT is the customer of a specific country bank. Accordingly, ING DIRECT has no need for a shared data platform across countries. Instead, ING DIRECT's operating model calls for a global brand offering simple high-value banking products to customers in different countries. To support this operating model, ING DIRECT has built a digitized platform consisting of a set of standard bank products, business processes, and IT infrastructure and systems that is replicated across country banks.

ING DIRECT offers a limited number of products, including savings accounts, mortgages, certificates of deposit, and a handful of mutual funds. Its formula of high savings rates and low-cost loans continues to attract over $1 billion a month in new bank accounts.[7] Meanwhile, its low operating costs (0.43 percent of assets, as compared with 2.5 percent for a typical full-service bank) lead to year-over-year profitability increases even during difficult times for financial services institutions.

To maintain the ING DIRECT brand and to leverage scale and best practice, the nine country banks offer virtually the same set of products and services. Each country bank has implemented infrastructure locally, mostly according to global technology standards. Each country bank's digitized platform starts with that infrastructure and adds standard systems and business processes. These systems and processes cover core banking services (e.g., mutual funds, credit scoring, brokerage), customer relationship services (e.g., customer information and history, customer relationship management processes), external services (e.g., prospecting and payment), and channel services (i.e., technology-based services that connect back-end systems to customer-facing systems).

New products are proposed through the bankwide product committee. A thorough proposal process identifies products and channels with the greatest value to the entire bank.[8] Some of the product and process modules are developed locally, but ING DIRECT's central IT function has created standard interfaces so that, for the most part, modules can be made available across ING DIRECT's country banks. Country managers can decide which modules they would like to adopt and can customize applications, as necessary, to meet local regulations.

Martin Vonk, the bank's COO and CIO, notes that the heavy emphasis on replicating products, services, and processes across the country banks significantly reduces the firm's business analysis and implementation costs: "The big, big money [in IT] is in business analysis and implementation. And that is where horizontal links across countries are creating huge savings for all of us. That is why we can implement [our] systems in weeks—we never implement anything in years. Months is the maximum we are talking about."

ING DIRECT needs a platform of standard products, processes, and systems, whereas PepsiAmericas' operating model depends on integrated customer and product information. Other firms' operating models demand high levels of both integration and standardization. Swiss Reinsurance's management team defined just such a vision.

Swiss Reinsurance Company: Harmonizing Processes and Data

Founded in 1863, Swiss Reinsurance Company (Swiss Re) is the world's largest and most diversified reinsurance company and one of the world's most profitable firms in terms of profit per employee.[9] Operating out of 190 offices in over thirty countries, Swiss Re's 10,000 employees provide clients with reinsurance solutions for property and casualty, life, and health insurance.

Like many large global companies, Swiss Re grew by establishing regional businesses to meet the needs of its distributed client base. However, this regional approach led to variations in how Swiss Re performed core operations such as contract administration and asset management. These variations were reflected in the systems supporting their processes. In the late 1990s, then-CEO Walter Kielholz defined an operating model that called for meeting the needs of global customers and managing risk globally. Kielholz initiated development of a global operating model and digitized platform to standardize critical business processes and deliver globally integrated business information. The platform has three components:[10]

1. *Core business processes:* A set of approximately twenty high-level core processes, such as client relationship management, risk acquisition, risk pricing and risk structuring, deal proposal and deal management,

contract administration, claims management, technical accounting, and asset management.

2. *Common business systems:* Common systems and tools supporting the core business processes. Swiss Re was able to standardize approximately 80 percent of core processes and related IT applications.

3. *Integrated information capability:* Shared and globally defined data generated by the core processes. Access to this data helps management steer the firm's performance by analyzing the impact of individual decisions on revenues, risks, capital, costs, and other key metrics.

Swiss Re's head of asset management notes that the digitized platform transformed the asset management business by providing "a consolidated picture of what on earth our investment result was, what it looked like, what the value of our assets was from an accounting and from a market value point of view. We also then were able to use it to feed our risk management engines and various other things, which allowed us effectively to take the second step, to run the portfolio in a consolidated way on a global basis."[11]

The head of product development notes that Swiss Re's platform allows the firm to compare profitability of the business across the globe on a real-time basis. This transparency, he notes, "allows us to say, 'We should write more of that and less of this.'" Swiss Re is still building its digitized platform, but its implementation of digitized core business processes and related data supports an end-to-end value chain.

HOW TO ARTICULATE AN OPERATING MODEL FOR YOUR FIRM

The four examples demonstrate the different choices for your operating model and the requisite digitized platforms. These platforms differ significantly in the kinds of capabilities they provide.

If you want to make IT a strategic asset, the first thing you have to do is define and then communicate an operating model. The operating model requires that business leaders make just two decisions about a firm's ongoing operations: (1) how much to standardize business processes, and (2) how much to integrate business processes.

Choosing Among Four Operating Model Options

Defining an operating model is a senior management responsibility. To support a senior-level discussion on your firm's operating model, we suggest you choose among four operating models, corresponding to the four examples in this chapter. Figure 2-1 summarizes the four alternative operating models.

The four operating models and the requirements for their accompanying digitized platforms are as follows:

- *Diversification:* Low standardization, low integration— involves building a platform of shared services that supports autonomous business entities (e.g., P&G).

- *Coordination:* Low standardization, high integration— involves building a platform of shared data to support integrated management decisions or a single face to the customer (e.g., PepsiAmericas).

FIGURE 2-1

Four operating model choices

	Coordination	Unification
High	■ Unique businesses with a need to know each other's transactions and relationships ■ Key platform capability: easy access to shared data for customer service, decision making, and integration	■ Single business with global process standards and shared global data ■ Key platform capability: standard business processes and global data access
	Diversification	**Replication**
Low	■ Independent businesses with different customers and expertise ■ Key platform capability: provide economies of scale through shared services without limiting independence	■ Independent but similar business units ■ Key platform capability: standard business processes and systems for global efficiencies
	Low	High

Business process integration *(vertical axis)*

Business process standardization *(horizontal axis)*

Source: © 2009 MIT Sloan Center for Information Systems Research. Used with permission.

- *Replication:* High standardization, low integration—involves building a platform of standard technologies and business processes to define a common brand (e.g., ING DIRECT and CEMEX).

- *Unification:* High standardization, high integration—involves building a platform of standardized technologies, business processes, and shared data to support global end-to-end customer requirements (e.g., Swiss Re and UPS package delivery).[12]

By reducing the operating model decision to these four options, you can focus management attention on the strategic implications of your IT decisions. You can make sure that your IT investments contribute to a digitized platform that enhances your firm's ability to operate how you want it to operate.

Small firms can usually identify an operating model and start to build a single digitized process platform to support that operating model. More complex firms need two, three, or more operating models—one at each organizational level (e.g., firmwide, business units, geography) where you want to share platform capabilities.[13]

Deploying Operating Models at Different Organizational Levels

Pharmaceutical giant Pfizer has strong functions.[14] Its three major business entities reflect these functions: R&D, manufacturing, and marketing. Both business objectives and regulatory requirements demand that Pfizer link its three major entities with seamless transaction data so that the firm can track its product. Thus, at an enterprise level the firm can benefit from a coordination model. Each of the entities, however, can choose a different operating model. Manufacturing, for example, might adopt a unification operating model. Adopting a unification model would simultaneously focus management attention on replicating best practices across Pfizer's plants to consistently meet safety standards while developing transparent data to facilitate global supply chain processes.

Figure 2-2 shows the target operating models of one of the banks we worked with—the most profitable bank in its region in 2007. This bank, like most banks, has three major business

FIGURE 2-2

Target operating model of a leading full-service bank

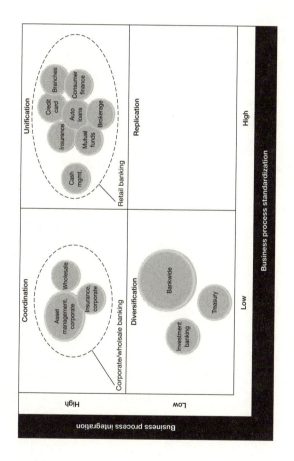

groups: retail, wholesale/corporate, and other (e.g., treasury and investment banking). These groups have very different products and business processes and few shared customers. At the enterprise level, the bank has adopted a diversification model sharing a few services such as HR, legal, risk, and some IT.

Wholesale/corporate banking thrives on a small set of customers with high-value relationships. To encourage local customization and innovation, the bank has not instituted standard business processes. However, the bank insists upon cross-selling, risk management by customer, and providing an integrated customer experience. The coordination model is perfect for this approach to operating the business.

In contrast, the treasury and investment banking group represents diverse business needs. The bank is happy to let the groups grow the individual lines of business autonomously, using the firm's shared services—a diversification model.

Finally, the retail group encompasses many product lines, including credit cards, checking, mortgages, loans, and insurance. The head of retail banking wants to encourage customers to "buy" as many retail products as possible. His concern is thus cross-selling and integrated customer service. To date he has met these objectives with a coordination operating model.

The bank's management team discussed how well the firm's operating model meets customer needs. The head of retail concluded that he needs to deliver lower costs than competitors on products that are essentially commodities. To do so, he will need a single, integrated retail banking platform that has a single process, across all products, for business processes such as opening a customer account, credit scoring, closing an account, and managing a relationship. Thus, he has started moving the entire retail business to a unification model (as shown in the figure) through a core banking system renewal project.

Putting a Stake in the Ground

All four operating models present opportunities to grow profitably. The choice of operating model, however, is a critical decision because it establishes the high-level requirements for your digitized platform. Thus, the operating model has important implications for your firm's ability to integrate acquisitions, expand into new markets, introduce a new product line, and compete on the basis of cost.

The diversification model foregoes some economies to maximize the opportunities created by local autonomy. The coordination model empowers individuals with information while resisting the impulse to dictate how they respond to that information. The replication model establishes a consistent brand identity across entities while choosing not to integrate their operations via common data. The unification model maximizes efficiencies and global reach while limiting variability.

Moving from the bottom left to the top right quadrant of figure 2-1 significantly increases the size and capability of the platform. In diversification, the most a firm typically will share is technology services and business support services such as HR, finance, and purchasing. In coordination, the firm adds common data to diversification platform requirements, whereas replication adds standardized core business processes to the diversification platform. In unification, the firm combines all the standard and shared elements of the other three operating models: technology, core business processes, firmwide data, and shared support processes.

The industry in which you operate will probably influence your choice of an operating model, but industry is unlikely to dictate what will work best for you. For example, Federal Express adopted a coordination model to compete against UPS's highly effective unification model for package delivery. The reasons for the different approaches are largely historical. UPS grew up with a large fleet of trucks. Federal Express started as an air express business that later acquired a ground delivery company. Instead of pursuing unification, Federal Express has turned the coordination model into an asset, offering customized services that are harder for a unification company to introduce.[15]

Selecting an operating model is a commitment to a way of doing business. That can be a daunting choice, but it's not possible to build a digitized platform without choosing an operating model. And choosing an operating model pays off. Relative to all others, firms with a strong digitized platform have 17 percent greater alignment between the strategic capabilities they claim they need and the capabilities they have implemented—a metric positively correlated with profitability.[16] These firms also reported higher operational efficiency (31 percent), customer intimacy (33 percent), product leadership (34 percent), and strategic agility (29 percent).[17]

In contrast, a firm without a digitized platform is slower to respond to new market opportunities. With each new strategic initiative, the firm must effectively begin anew. So, with each new initiative, cost and complexity mount, resulting in IT and business process spaghetti.

IDENTIFYING WHAT'S STABLE TO MAKE WAY FOR CHANGE

Defining an operating model requires putting a stake in the ground and committing to how your firm will operate in the future. But the key to implementing an effective operating model is not a matter of understanding how your business will change. What IT-savvy firms do extraordinarily well is to recognize what is *not* changing. Every viable business can find something stable about how it generates sales and profits.

By defining what is stable about your firm's business processes and choosing an operating model, you establish the integration and standardization requirements for a digitized platform. This platform takes the inefficiencies and inconsistencies out of your operations and enables innovation. With a digitized platform, your customer-facing people can focus on meeting the needs of customers without having to worry whether their information is correct or whether operations will deliver to expectations.

As you ponder your operating model, here are some dos and don'ts to consider.

Do

- Specify one operating model for each level in your firm where you report performance (e.g., firmwide, geographies, product groups, customer segments).[18]

- Drive the choice of operating model by how you fundamentally want to profit and grow.

- Make the operating model language part of your firm's daily conversation. Every major firm decision (e.g., budgets, hiring, bonuses, strategic planning, outsourcing, new product launches) is an opportunity to reinforce and further implement your model.

- Involve IT management in the operating model decision. IT leadership will be a driving force in building the digitized platform supporting the operating model.

- Identify who will be accountable for designing and building the digitized platform.

Don't

- Assume business processes must be different just because they always have been. Business entities can apply different decision rules (e.g., pricing algorithms, commission rules) using the same business process.

- Ignore real differences. In particular, developing markets can require very different operations from established markets.

- Underestimate the task. The only way to implement an operating model is through effective allocation of decision rights and accountabilities.

- Make the operating model decision lightly. This is a decision that dictates ongoing investment priorities for years.

- Think operating models only affect IT—they affect everyone.

Operating models should not change very often. But when management decides to introduce a new operating model, the change will be far-reaching. In addition to technology and business processes, people's roles, incentives, and even the culture of the organization will be affected. Please debate how your firm wants to operate. Deciding on your operating model will provide the direction for all the IT decisions in your firm.

With a clear operating model, you're now ready for the biggest challenge in IT: your IT funding model. That's the topic of the next chapter.

Revamping Your IT Funding Model

Do you believe your business spent about the right amount of money on IT last year? Do you believe your business allocated that IT spending in about the right places? Do you believe your business got about the right returns from its spending on IT? If you didn't answer yes to all three questions, it's time to revisit your IT funding model.

IT funding decisions are important because as systems are implemented, they become part of your firm's legacy. Their ongoing support requires time and money. More important, systems influence, constrain, or dictate how business processes are performed. So think of IT funding decisions as long-term strategic decisions that implement your firm's operating model.

In other words, IT funding decisions are a senior management responsibility.

Despite the strategic implications of IT funding decisions, we have found that senior managers are often reluctant to make them. When senior executives abdicate responsibility for IT funding decisions, IT executives or business units are usually left to set the priorities. Often, individual business units approve and fund hundreds of business cases, leaving the IT unit to act as a referee or valiantly attempt to deliver on all of the projects. The result is a backlog of delayed initiatives and a set of systems with dubious business value and high support costs—clear evidence that the IT funding model is broken.

It is nearly impossible to get value from IT if your IT funding model is broken. How do you fix it? This chapter examines the set of interrelated factors composing an effective IT funding model: both the processes that can make it effective and a way to assess the risks and rewards of alternative IT investments. First, let's discuss the business transformation at BT, one of the world's largest telecommunications companies. One of BT's first steps in its transformation was to revamp its IT funding model.

FUNDING BT'S TRANSFORMATION

When Ben Verwaayen arrived at BT as its new CEO in 2002, BT was suffering the effects of the Internet bust. The company was saddled with debt from a rapid expansion during the preceding boom years and was facing a newly competitive telephony environment. Verwaayen restructured around three lines of business: retail, wholesale, and global services. His goal was to transform BT from a traditional telco to a global leader in networked IT services.[1]

Verwaayen believed that all BT services should have the same "taste, look, and feel" and that the customer experience should be the same regardless of the point of contact with BT. He stressed the importance of carefully managing costs across the businesses while simultaneously finding new sources of revenue. Verwaayen expected IT to be a critical tool for enabling BT's business transformation. He formed the IT board, a group of thirteen business and IT leaders responsible for IT investment decisions. In its quarterly meetings, the IT board sets direction for IT, establishes funding priorities, and monitors the return on investment (ROI) of strategic projects.

In 2004, Verwaayen brought in Al-Noor Ramji as CIO. At the time, BT had over 4,000 systems, and its more than 6,000 IT employees were working on over 4,300 projects. Ramji noted that the company's IT environment was not designed for integration or low cost. He established "One IT for One BT" to consolidate the systems environment and reduce the project portfolio. He reorganized BT's project portfolio, targeting BT's three core business processes: lead-to-cash ("selling stuff"), trouble-to-resolve ("fixing stuff"), and concept-to-market ("innovating stuff"). These three processes defined the key elements of BT's unification operating model and provided the focus for IT spending and resource allocation.

Ramji introduced a disciplined business case process for IT funding decisions. In this process, the lines of business prepare a business case detailing the specific business benefits of a new initiative, while the IT group provides input on costs, technology options, alternative approaches, and time frames. As a rule, all business cases must demonstrate an acceptable ROI. Not all business initiatives can meet an ROI hurdle, however. Some business initiatives are foundational or mandated by regulations or have hard-to-quantify benefits. In these cases, Ramji requires that the proposer obtain CEO sign-off. Direct requests to the CEO are sometimes necessary, but they are rare, in part because they require an investment of the proposer's political capital.

The business case process does not end when a project is approved. Projects must demonstrate their viability at various stages throughout development. A project is initiated at a three-day off-site meeting called a hothouse, in which business and IT program team members, including customers, determine the scope of the program. Within ten days of completing the hothouse, they finalize the formal business case, prioritize resources, and designate funding. They also establish the metrics for regular reviews. Then, every ninety days, a central team reviews each program against the objectives and metrics determined in the hothouse. BT's finance team can choose to cancel any project if it fails to meet established objectives and metrics. The results of the reviews are published on BT's internal Web site. These reviews continue beyond implementation, when a post-implementation review establishes the success of the initiative in generating expected business returns.

As a result of these and other changes, BT has consolidated its systems environment and has built a digitized platform to support lead-to-cash, the first of its three key processes. The firm reduced its total IT costs by 14 percent and cut the unit cost of IT services while tripling output and doubling delivery speed. Best of all, BT's new IT funding process has facilitated the firm's transformation into a business that can compete with Google and Amazon in providing digitized services and business processes to the marketplace.

BT has found that the new IT funding process has helped promote learning. For example, hothouses required business and IT people to make big changes in how they deliver systems. By the time all programs went through their second ninety-day cycle, however, most business and IT managers at BT had become comfortable with the process. The regular reviews are putting more emphasis on driving benefits from current projects. At the same time, participants can see what metrics and outcomes are realistic and most relevant for achieving business objectives. This leads to better business cases over time. And better business cases generate higher-impact systems and processes, because people throughout the firm start to recognize what they should demand of IT-enabled business change initiatives. All this learning makes BT more IT savvy.

THE IT-SAVVY APPROACH TO IT FUNDING

Like all firms, IT-savvy firms find IT investment decisions challenging. They have more opportunities to invest in IT than they have funds (or attention) to invest. But as BT demonstrates, the IT funding models at IT-savvy firms have three important components. First, senior executives *establish clear priorities and criteria* for their IT investments. Second, management *develops a transparent process* for assessing potential projects and allocating resources. Third, management *monitors the impacts of prior investment decisions* and uses that learning to guide future investments.

This is not an easy list of practices to implement. Now add strong personalities, coalitions, political agendas, reorganizations, and tenderly massaged numbers. Despite the challenges, IT-savvy firms relentlessly pursue these practices and learn from each experience. Over time, their adherence to these principles delivers continuous improvement in their funding processes and the resulting systems. Let's explore each practice.

Establishing Clear Priorities and Criteria

The starting point for your funding priorities is your operating model (chapter 2). Your operating model clarifies your strategic operating priorities and, by default, your IT priorities. BT further defined its priorities by clarifying three core business processes (lead-to-cash, trouble-to-resolve, and concept-to-market). Most of the IT-savvy firms we've studied have developed a similar list of business process priorities. These processes put meat on the bones of the operating model.

Not all firms frame their IT priorities in terms of end-to-end core processes. Southwest Airlines, the United States' largest airline in terms of passengers flown, used a similar concept, but different language. Southwest established IT funding priorities by focusing on its "sacred transactions"—those transactions capturing core operating data across the company. In late 2001,

Southwest's management recognized that the firm's systems environment was limiting its ability to adapt to market changes and serve its customers effectively. In reviewing its strategic requirements, management concluded that the firm's reservation system was at the heart of the company's sacred transactions and that it had become outdated. Thus, in mapping Southwest's business transformation, management listed the data and processes related to reservations as its top priority.[2]

Swiss Re, in contrast, focused on twenty core front office and back office activities, as described in chapter 2. This larger set of more narrowly defined activities is typical of how financial services institutions define their process priorities. What the BT, Southwest, and Swiss Re approaches have in common is that they create a focal point for business change efforts. The focal point helps target spending on high-value projects.

Ideally, you would focus all your investments on your key strategic initiatives. But, of course, you cannot avoid pressures to address externally imposed changes (e.g., new regulations), maintenance requirements (e.g., small changes to applications to keep them current and operating at acceptable response times), and competitive threats (e.g., the need to respond to a competitor's new digital customer service). Like BT's option for CEO sign-off, you will need a mechanism for addressing those demands. This is part of the transparent process for making funding decisions.

Developing a Transparent Prioritization Process

Once BT established its business process priorities, management defined the requirements for business cases and the criteria on which decisions would be based. IT-savvy firms regularly identify a senior leadership team with ultimate responsibility for IT prioritization. At a minimum, these senior management teams define core processes and strategic change initiatives. Where tensions exist among strategic priorities, these senior teams often make the call about which projects go forward and which are put on hold.

When firms are pursuing major change initiatives, they sometimes delegate a single executive—often the CIO—to set priorities to ensure that the initiative is fully funded over its life. When a major initiative is all-consuming, firms do not benefit much from protracted discussions of funding alternatives by senior management. Senior executive time is better spent leading the business change. This was the case at a health care consortium that was implementing an electronic medical record across its multiple hospitals—the CIO could simply take charge of defining the sequence of projects. However, if you are pursuing multiple strategic opportunities, you are more likely to need a committee of top executives, like at BT, to debate the alternatives and their implications for the firm.

Regardless of who ultimately makes prioritization decisions, top-performing firms are clear about the criteria for approved projects. These criteria specify what belongs in a business case and how project sponsors will be held accountable for the benefits they estimate in a business case.

Solid business cases require that the IT unit provide an estimate of ongoing IT support costs. For such costs to be meaningful, the IT department needs to create transparency regarding its unit costs (e.g., cost per fully supported laptop, cost per printed page, cost per data storage unit, cost for development). Many IT units have not completed the kind of activity-based costing exercise they need to help business people understand the ongoing costs of their initiatives. Unit cost tracking should be a high priority for every IT unit. If you don't know how much it costs to run and maintain your major applications and infrastructure services, you can bet you're spending too much.

Lack of a transparent process invariably leads to dysfunctional politics, as individuals look to influence people they think can help them get their projects approved. If you see project funding deals being made on the golf course or as part of a quid pro quo deal, you will know your process is not sufficiently transparent.

Monitoring the Impacts of Prior Investment Decisions

Getting value from IT is a learning process, and our research has repeatedly found that one of the most valuable tools for learning is a post-implementation review (PIR). Many firms have attempted to employ post-implementation reviews, but only 24 percent of firms report effective PIR programs.[3] A PIR adds value by transparently helping stakeholders understand where their estimates of potential value were wrong and how managers can drive more value from another similar initiative.[4]

BT's program of post-implementation reviews develops effective learning about the value obtained from each project and what's possible from the next project. BT has a central committee responsible for consistent PIR processes that compares the value generated and value estimated in each business case. BT's PIR process begins prior to development and continues every ninety days through implementation, so stakeholders can identify issues or concerns as they emerge.

IT-savvy firms use the PIR process to complete the IT funding cycle—from idea to implementation to value measurement to the next idea. Meanwhile, the transparent process eases the transition from project funding to project evaluation. Now is a good time for you to start ensuring that your IT funding approach has the three important components we find at IT-savvy firms. As BT found, it takes time to develop proficiency in these areas.

MANAGING YOUR IT PORTFOLIO

Establishing the processes to manage the IT funding is a necessary first step to getting value. But how can you judge whether, in total, the firm is allocating its spending appropriately? One way is to move the frame of reference (and thus the political football of IT prioritization) from the IT project to the IT portfolio. We have been focusing on the spending for IT projects that introduce new capabilities to a firm, but the average firm spends over two thirds of its IT budget just running and maintaining its existing systems. Often, it's the sustaining and maintaining part of the budget that leads executives to worry that they are not getting good value from IT. So the first step in managing an IT portfolio is to distinguish between two types of expenditures: project funding for new initiatives and operating budgets for sustaining IT.

IT Funding for New Versus Sustaining Initiatives

All IT spending falls into either the new or sustaining category. Sustaining expenditures keep the current systems running and include regular maintenance and updating—often called keeping the lights on. Sustaining outlays are typically viewed as nondiscretionary spending in firms. As a result, the sustaining spending can be a source of frustration. In 2007 the average firm spent 71 percent of its total IT spending (operating expenses plus capital) in the sustaining category.[5]

The remaining 29 percent of the average firm's IT spending was allocated to new business initiatives. New investment includes all new business initiatives and major changes to applications and business processes, including new IT infrastructure. Investments in new initiatives are typically approved as individual projects. To ensure those projects contribute to strategic priorities, growing numbers of firms are grouping projects into programs. The programs correspond to the firm's major change and platform building initiatives. Senior managers—often in business-IT pairs—lead these programs and coordinate multiple projects to achieve the objectives of their programs. At BT, Al-Noor Ramji and his colleagues assigned each project to one of twenty-nine programs, which supported various aspects of the firm's three key processes. Figure 3-1 shows how new and sustaining investments combine to create an IT portfolio.

Importantly, our statistical analyses show that firms allocating more of their IT spending to new rather than sustaining initiatives had significantly higher revenue growth and net

FIGURE 3-1

What's in the IT portfolio

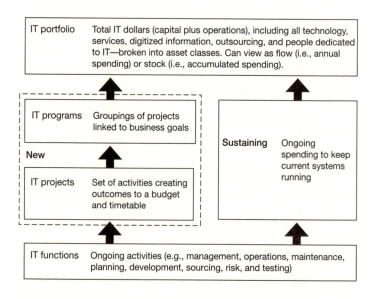

Source: © 2009 MIT Sloan Center for Information Systems Research. Used with permission.

margins relative to their competitors. But 32 percent of the large firms we studied spent more than 75 percent of their total IT dollars running existing systems. At some firms, sustaining investments were as high as 85 percent of IT investments. For various reasons, these non-IT-savvy firms are frittering away more of their IT dollars to stay in the same place. One of the roles of the IT funding model is to move this 75 percent to a more competitive level—say 60 percent—by looking for common solutions and consolidating the IT spaghetti that exists in many firms.[6]

Business leaders instinctively recognize the advantages of spending more on new projects and less on keeping the lights on. However, simply pulling the plug on nondiscretionary spending is not a good approach to reweighting your IT portfolio. If you want to reduce nondiscretionary IT spending, you'll need to reduce unnecessary variation in the business processes, technologies, and applications you're running. Portfolio management facilitates thinking about how you're allocating your IT spending.

The Risk-Return Profiles of Different Asset Classes

The IT portfolio takes a holistic view of the firm's IT spending.[7] Different categories of IT spending have different risk-return profiles.

Consider, for example, the different risk-return profiles of investments in expanding network capacity versus a business intelligence system. The expansion in network capacity may be driven by an assessment of the risks of not making the investment, such as increasing system downtime or unacceptable response times for customer service. Also, limited network capacity could delay a new business initiative that required lots of bandwidth (e.g., services incorporating video). In contrast, a new business intelligence application could generate business returns by enabling improved capability to identify new markets or services if the insights identified are successfully monetized. A key risk for business intelligence is that the returns might not significantly exceed the cost of system implementation and operation.

Effective portfolio management recognizes major differences in the objectives of a firm's IT investments, so that individual investments are evaluated according to their different objectives. Portfolio thinking helps firms avoid a one-size-fits-all approach to prioritizing projects. A quarter of *Fortune* 1000 firms have adopted IT portfolio management, and there is evidence of a payoff. One study found that the 18 percent of firms with the most sophisticated IT portfolio management processes also have higher profitability.[8]

The IT portfolio divides a firm's IT investments into asset classes with different risk-return profiles—just as cash, bonds, real estate, and various types of equity investments offer different risk-return profiles in your financial portfolio. There are a number of ways to classify IT investments into asset classes, and firms typically tailor their asset classes to match the language they use for management decision making.

Figure 3-2 shows a set of four asset classes for an IT portfolio, developed at MIT's Center for Information Systems Research (CISR). We collect benchmarks each year on these four asset classes:

- *Strategic IT:* Increase sales and conduct business experiments.

- *Informational IT:* Provide information for management.

- *Transactional IT:* Cut business costs though automation.

- *IT infrastructure:* Provide a shared base of IT services.

Strategic IT investments focus on business experiments. These investments are risky—they respond to new business

FIGURE 3-2

Risks and returns of IT investment asset classes

IT asset class[a]		Type of IT investment	Risk-return characteristics[b]	Analogy to personal investment portfolio
	Strategic	Supports new market entry, new product development, strategic experiments using IT (e.g., bank ATMs)	Correlated to more sales from customized products. Highest risk, large potential upside, and 50% failure rate.	Emerging markets
	Infrastructure	Provides the foundation of shared IT services (both technical and human) used by multiple applications (e.g., servers, networks, laptops, shared customer databases)	Correlated to increased market value and higher short-term cost. Moderate risk due to long life and business and technical uncertainty.	Options plus real estate
	Informational	Provides information for managing, accounting, reporting, and communicating internally and with customers, suppliers, and regulators (e.g., sales analysis or SOX)	Correlated to higher profit margins. Moderate risk due to difficulty of acting on information to create business value.	Broad market index fund (e.g., S&P 500)
	Transactional	Automates business processes, cuts costs, or increases the volume of business a firm can conduct per unit cost (e.g., billing, insurance renewal)	Strongly correlated to lower business costs. Lowest risk, with solid return of 25–40%.	Bonds

Increasing risk

Source: © 2009 MIT Sloan Center for Information Systems Research. Used with permission.

a. A single project may be any combination of more than one asset class.

b. Statistically significant impacts on firm performance, controlling for industry size and firm differences.

opportunities in ways that require developing new capabilities. Firms can experiment with new channels, new electronic customer services, and new electronic linkages with partners. About half of all strategic investments fail, so the justification—and the post-implementation review process—for projects in this asset class needs to assess the full set of strategic investments rather than individual projects.

Informational IT investments provide information for financial reporting, compliance, communication, analysis, and managerial decision making. Informational investments provide information for internal communication and analysis (e.g., sales analysis) and external communication (e.g., providing product information to customers). Informational investments also include IT for most regulatory compliance. Regulatory compliance investments are necessary, but firms should be looking for ways to invest in value-adding capabilities rather than consistently slapping another layer of applications on an already complex set of systems.

Transactional investments cut costs or increase throughput for the same cost (e.g., think of a brokerage firm's trade processing system). Transactional investments automate business processes, reducing complexity and cost. They typically have strongly positive ROI-based business cases and are the least risky of the IT asset classes.

Infrastructure investments are the foundation of the IT portfolio. The justification for these investments is sometimes cost reduction. Investments that standardize and consolidate technologies should reduce nondiscretionary spending. But some infrastructure investments will provide new capabilities (such as investments in voice over IP or mobile technologies). These investments are options for the future, but, once implemented, they will both increase sustaining expenditures and potentially enable faster time to market. In addition, the IT unit will identify preventive investments, much like government investments in rebuilding roads and bridges. As firms become more technology intensive, management needs to commit to an ongoing renewal of the firm's infrastructure assets.

Because these asset classes offer very different risks and returns, portfolio management helps a firm monitor and adjust IT investments according to management's performance objectives. Figure 3-2 summarizes the financial impact of investments in each of the four asset classes using the analogy to asset classes in a personal investment portfolio. Understanding the risk-return profiles of the asset classes will allow you to more confidently make trade-offs at budget time. As a result of the benefits of their practices such as PIR, IT-savvy firms have lower risk even in the more risky asset classes such as strategic and infrastructure investments. Thus, IT-savvy firms can confidently invest more in IT and weight their IT portfolios to the more risky asset classes.

The key to effective IT portfolio management is to review your intended IT investments by asset class. Take into account your strategic goals, the risk-return profile of the IT asset classes, and how IT savvy you are today and ask: Is this the right mix for us? Or do we need more cost saving or strategic investments this year? EMC has used portfolio management to simultaneously enable enterprisewide customer service and local business unit innovations.

PORTFOLIO MANAGEMENT AT EMC

EMC, a high-tech company with 40,000 employees world-wide, designs, builds, and sells storage systems, software, and services to store, protect, and leverage information.[9] EMC has four principal business segments: information storage, content management and archiving, information security, and virtual infrastructure. In 2008, EMC's net profit margin was 9 percent, compared with an industry average of 3.4 percent. Its revenues grew 19 percent in 2007, to $13.2 billion, and 12 percent in 2008, to $14.9 billion.

As EMC's revenues were growing dramatically, so were its systems. With approximately forty acquisitions since 2003, the systems landscape became very complex. A senior IT leader at EMC reflected that "spending money was easy and we didn't have a holistic view."

EMC has been developing its portfolio management processes since 2001. Each business unit has a process and portfolio management (PPMG) organization, consisting mainly of process-oriented IT people. The PPMG organization manages demand and optimizes the portfolio for the business unit. In addition, PPMG units interact with the central IT organization, which provides application development, infrastructure services, and security.

At the enterprise level, management focuses on three categories of IT investments (figure 3-3). The first two refer to EMC's two core processes: requisition-to-cash (the general and administrative portfolio) and lead-to-service (the customer operations portfolio). The third category, the IT portfolio,

FIGURE 3-3

IT portfolio management at EMC

"IT is the business partner you turn to, to get to a common platform."

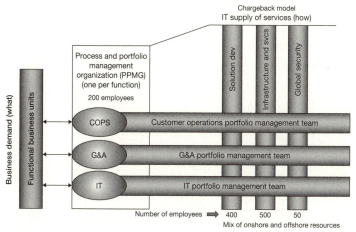

Benefits
- Improved identification and redesign of processes in support of technology deployment
- Clear understanding of how to use IT services
- Increased control provided to business for setting priorities and acquiring necessary funding
- Funding controlled by business functions
- Centrally managed service levels at lowest possible costs

Source: EMC documents and interviews with EMC executives.

captures other centralized IT investments. An IT steering committee (with the CIO, executive vice presidents, and senior vice presidents as members) establishes strategic priorities and oversees the enterprisewide portfolio. A rigorous business case process is used to allocate central IT resources to business unit demands and to ensure that both business unit and enterprisewide goals are met.

At EMC, portfolio management has enabled an increasingly complex firm to balance business unit and enterprise IT demands. EMC has reduced its number of IT applications from 600 to 450. IT has also improved management of suppliers and vendors, reduced consulting costs, and eliminated shadow IT groups (the IT organizations created by business units to circumvent central IT). Now IT investment is based on quantitative measures of success—a hugely important change given that IT constitutes around 16 percent of EMC's capital budget.

The change to IT portfolio management helped rationalize IT investments and free up IT funds for more strategic spending. EMC lowered its total IT spending in 2006 to 3.1 percent of revenues (relative to an industry average of 5.3 percent). EMC's investment allocations are now 23 percent strategic (double the industry average of 11 percent), 20 percent informational (industry average: 18 percent), 23 percent transactional (industry average: 25 percent), and 34 percent infrastructure (industry average: 46 percent).[10] Consolidation of infrastructure and applications freed up funds for strategic investments while reducing the overall IT spending.

Perhaps the most valuable outcome of portfolio management is that 80 percent of the new initiatives budget goes to enterprise initiatives. This has given EMC a single view of customers and products across business units. The remaining 20 percent of the budget for new initiatives goes toward local business unit innovation. Ken LeBlanc, senior director, IT Business Operations, summed up EMC's experience: "Embracing portfolio management and the underlying governance has enabled us to consistently align IT budget and resources to the right business priorities. Prior to this we were unable to accurately measure the effectiveness of IT investments and direct contribution to EMC's business process."

THE BENEFITS OF FIXING WHAT'S BROKEN

In these last two chapters, we argued that firms cannot generate business value from IT if they have not clarified their operating model or if their IT funding model is not working. This is why the first obsession of the IT-savvy firm is to fix what's broken. Once you take charge of directing IT funding to strategic business needs, you are ready for the second obsession: to build a digitized platform for enhanced business performance. In fact, you have started the journey to platform digitization. The next chapter describes that journey.

Building a Digitized Platform

Most of us remember the journey from adolescence to adulthood as a mix of pain and anxiety with enough triumphs and good times to keep us plowing ahead. Building a digitized platform is a similar journey—with perhaps a little more willingness than the average teenager to take input from those who have traveled the journey before. Only this time, you're taking your hundreds, thousands, or tens of thousands of colleagues with you on a journey toward disciplined, world-class, end-to-end business processes. We refer to this adventure as your IT savvy journey.

Building a digitized platform is the second obsession of IT-savvy firms. It's a journey that leads to greater returns per

IT dollar invested. You will acquire a great deal of learning along the way to a digitized platform. This chapter describes that learning and the different stages of development. The next chapter talks about the IT governance you need to institutionalize the necessary learning.

SWISS RE'S IT SAVVY JOURNEY

Firms share many common experiences as they move toward increased IT savvy. Swiss Re provides a good example.[1]

Swiss Re was founded in 1863. Like many large global companies, it had grown by establishing regional businesses to meet the needs of its distributed client base, but this regional approach meant that each region designed its own processes and supported its own systems. By the late 1990s, when Swiss Re wanted to manage risk and customer relationships globally, the legacy of local systems and processes proved a major obstacle.

Swiss Re addressed this obstacle by building a digitized platform that consists of three layers: (1) infrastructure technologies, (2) core business processes and applications, and (3) firmwide integrated data. Swiss Re built these layers one at a time.

The journey started in the mid-1990s. First, CIO Yury Zaytsev initiated efforts to build a shared IT infrastructure, consolidate data centers, and enhance IT governance. The result of these efforts was lower IT costs and increased IT unit professionalism.

By 2000, Zaytsev had started working with business leaders to develop common systems for its processes. The IT unit identified a great deal of variability across the business groups. For example, Swiss Re had thirty-five client management systems and twenty-five underwriting systems, which meant that the firm had at least thirty-five different client management processes and twenty-five different underwriting processes. Eventually business leaders took over responsibility for defining global processes. These leaders worked with IT to implement global systems and establish common processes.

By 2005, the company had implemented common systems for about twenty global processes, and Swiss Re's focus shifted to data integration. The data integration effort allowed straight-through processing of sets of digitized processes. Sylvia Steinmann, CIO of Swiss Re's financial services group, explained the impact: "Today in asset management we have this completely straight-through processing. From the order management system, we have a straight-through process for settlement of the trades. Once they settle, we have straight-through processing for dividend payments and for interest payments. There's little human intervention."

Producing this kind of straight-through, globally common process was a long, and sometimes arduous, journey. Frequently, professionals at Swiss Re found the new global systems harder to use than the old ones they knew well. In some cases, it took almost two years for individuals to stop regretting what they had lost and learn how to maximize the increased value of the information from the new systems. But the benefits have easily quashed the concerns of doubters. Christoph Menn, head of product development and strategy, described the reaction this way: "Immediately after the rollout of global tools and systems some may have perceived that as now having less . . . flexibility. However, the new pricing tools provided them with much better and consistent analytics to assess the business, and over time, that second aspect won out."

Learning to drive benefits from—and consistently extend—a powerful digitized platform has numerous challenges, but the payback can be substantial. Despite difficult economic times, Swiss Re has been able to use its digitized platform to introduce product innovations and new partnerships. As Swiss Re and other financial services firms struggle to recover from the 2008 financial crisis, a world-class digitized platform will reduce costs and provide critical decision making information.[2]

THE JOURNEY HAS FOUR STAGES

We have summarized the IT experiences of many firms as a journey with four stages (figure 4-1).[3] The four stages are as follows:

1. *Localizing:* Firms rapidly grow new systems as they respond to customer demands and seek to establish their unique value proposition.

2. *Standardizing:* Firms retreat from the expense of rapid-fire responses and look for IT efficiencies through technology standardization and shared infrastructure.

FIGURE 4-1

The IT savvy journey

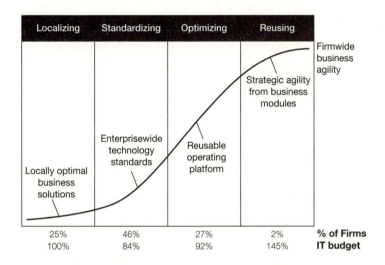

Localizing	Standardizing	Optimizing	Reusing

Firmwide business agility

Strategic agility from business modules

Enterprisewide technology standards

Reusable operating platform

Locally optimal business solutions

25%	46%	27%	2%	**% of Firms**
100%	84%	92%	145%	**IT budget**

Source: Based on a figure from J. Ross, P. Weill, and D. Robertson, *Enterprise Architecture as Strategy: Creating a Foundation for Business Execution* (Boston: Harvard Business School Press, 2006). The data at the base is from a 2007 MIT CISR survey of 1,508 firms (53 percent from the United States).

3. *Optimizing:* Firms implement disciplined enterprise processes and shared data as prescribed by their operating model.

4. *Reusing:* Firms start to think of their business processes as reusable components that they can customize for new, but related, business opportunities.

These four stages represent the organizational learning that enables large, complex firms to achieve simplification and agility. The stages also capture the path that newer, fast-growing firms face as they settle into defined business models. There is good news and bad news inherent to these stages.

First, the bad news: particularly at large, older firms, each stage can last an extended period of time. We've followed some firms that have labored in the second stage for many years. And it is clear to us from watching firms try and fail that *you cannot skip a stage*—at least, not without paying a big price.

The good news is that firms understanding their path to a digitized platform can get increased value from their IT-enabled business initiatives right away. Those benefits will increase every day. And because most firms are still in the throes of the earlier stages, you have time to do this right.

Therefore, you'll want to make sure you understand the nature of the stage you're in, how you can drive benefits from that stage, and how you should position yourself to move aggressively to the next stage.

Stage 1: Localizing

The first stage describes the dynamic, innovative approach of a new firm or business unit. The firm's priority is rapid growth in a new industry or expansion into new markets. The firm's niche that distinguishes it from competitors is emerging, so it is experimenting, looking for a sustainable value proposition. Thus the long-term system and process requirements are unclear. This stage leads to a constant stream of new systems addressing new opportunities. This stage also describes localized systems being built in large organizations in which individual business units independently develop whatever they need.

Stage 1 benefits. Firms can generate enormous business value in stage 1. For example, investment banks were long comfortable in stage 1 because the emphasis of their systems efforts was to develop new products. They were less concerned with integrating the processes across the firm. Eventually, the focus on products limits the ability to service the needs of a customer across products, but a stage 1 investment bank can generate huge profits from rapid introduction of new financial instruments.

Similarly, companies in new industries often belong in stage 1 because they have to test their value proposition. When the logistics industry was taking shape in the early 1990s, new companies created IT-based services to support their first customers. Because they did not fully understand how they would make money, logistics firms focused on responding to the unique needs of every new customer. They did not—indeed, they could not—focus on implementing disciplined processes and systems.

Whereas some firms (or parts of firms) are in stage 1 of their IT savvy journey because it's the right fit for them, many others are in stage 1 because they haven't recognized that stage 1 runs its course and eventually makes IT a strategic liability. One-off and redundant solutions create a legacy of systems that cannot talk to each other. The spaghetti pictured in figure 1-1 is a good representation of the typical systems environment in stage 1 firms. The rapid responses to new opportunities lead to a legacy that limits responsiveness going forward.

Many IT professionals are quite adept at making disparate systems look integrated, but the code required to link applications becomes increasingly complex. Over time, key systems have so many links to other systems that even small changes are time-consuming, expensive, and risky. Meanwhile, individuals in the firm find a variety of ways to work around systems so they can meet customer needs. Soon business processes lack consistency and performance gaps become commonplace.

Transitioning from stage 1 to stage 2. Around 25 percent of the firms we've studied are in the localizing stage.[4] Most will eventually move on—or risk being outperformed by more efficient competitors. Cost is usually the stimulus prompting firms to move forward. More traditionally lucrative industries, such as investment banking and pharmaceuticals, have been slower to abandon the localizing stage but are moving now. New industries will continue to join their ranks.

The transition from stage 1 to stage 2 is often initiated by the CEO or CFO. One day the CEO or CFO wakes up knowing the firm is spending too much on IT. How he or she knows is not clear. For some leaders it's a gut feeling—good management instincts. For others it's formal IT benchmarking or informal comparisons with peers in other firms. Some take note of increasing IT budgets. Still others become alarmed by the growing number of breaks in service caused by the complexity of the systems environment.

At this point, management recognizes some of the signs of a broken funding model or lack of operating model, as described in the preceding two chapters. The ensuing action is quite predictable: the CIO (often, a newly appointed CIO) receives an order to fix IT and reduce costs by 15 percent (or pick your own number). If the firm has learned how to manage IT-enabled change, the transition to stage 2 will yield immediate benefits. Here are some signs that the firm has learned the important lessons from stage 1 and is ready to deliver on the benefits of later stages:

- Individual systems promise a positive ROI, and business managers deliver on that promise, . . . but no one is assessing the impacts of IT on the enterprise as a whole.

- The firm has many good systems, . . . but a greater percentage of the IT spending each year is required to maintain those systems.

- The CIO or IT director works with business unit, product line, or functional leaders to meet their needs, . . . but delivery is too slow.

- Senior management has confidence in the CIO's ability to lead . . . *and* is ready to support CIO initiatives.

Stage 2: Standardizing

Following the initial growth stage, firms look to ward off competitors. Discipline and cost cutting become priorities. In stage 2 the IT unit introduces IT standards to limit IT costs and risks, and senior management commits to a shared infrastructure. The shared infrastructure introduces economies of scale and opportunities to integrate systems. Standardizing firms we studied were spending about 84 percent of what localizing firms were spending on IT. Forty-six percent of the firms were in the standardizing stage.

Stage 2 benefits. The most apparent benefit of the second stage is IT cost savings. As in the first stage, the role of IT is to automate local business processes. However, IT management expands its focus from concerns about the functionality of individual applications to include the cost effectiveness and reliability of the firm's IT portfolio. Management examines the portfolio to determine the relative weighting of sustaining versus new initiative outlays.

The cost savings in stage 2 result from efforts to standardize and consolidate technologies, sometimes after a merger. Rebecca Rhoads, Raytheon's global CIO, described the standardizing effort at Raytheon after a merger of five companies: "We went from 150 payroll systems to one, 28 e-mail systems to one; just brutal, brutal, huge, huge mountains that needed to be moved. We reduced IT spend by over 40 percent. That's what we needed to do over the first three to four years."[5]

Because technology standardization reduces the number of technologies the IT unit must support, stage 2 leads to lower IT risks. Meanwhile, business unit sharing of infrastructure services lowers the costs of IT services such as support, maintenance, and purchasing. Technology standardization also enhances IT security and accelerates IT development time. And because technology standardization demands world-class IT processes, stage 2 enhances the professionalism of the IT staff. These staff members are in a position to add greater business value because the more standardized environment reduces the time spent addressing niggling technology problems.

The migration to a standardized technology environment fundamentally changes a firm's approach to systems delivery. Instead of defining a solution and looking for technology that best delivers that solution, firms in this stage negotiate the best solution available that meets the firm's standards. In well-managed stage 2 companies, there is also an exception process that makes sure the firm recognizes when standards are outdated or incapable of meeting important, strategic needs.

Standardizing technology, however, does not readily overcome the stage 1 problem of data redundancy and inaccessibility. Thus, although standardizing technology enhances IT efficiency, it does not make IT a strategic asset.

Transitioning from stage 2 to stage 3. Firms that complete the second stage of the IT savvy journey achieve significant cost savings and reliability. The resulting systems landscape is simpler and easier to maintain. Thus, they reduce the proportion of IT funding allocated to sustaining existing systems. Here is how a firm knows it has realized the benefits from stage 2 and is ready for stage 3:

- A standard set of technology infrastructure services meets the needs of the firm, with only a few exceptions.

- Management has introduced funding mechanisms to build and support shared infrastructure.

- IT unit costs (e.g., cost per laptop, e-mail, storage, or help desk response) are in steady decline, and IT spending as a percentage of revenues is low by industry standards.

- Senior managers support the constraints—and understand the benefits—of technology standardization.

- The firm has introduced a productive exception process to ensure that standards do not hinder business success.

- But . . . the firm's business operations are not world-class.

Stage 3: Optimizing

In the third stage, firms look to reduce business operating costs and ensure high-quality customer services. Depending on their choice of operating model, firms vary on how much they emphasize standard processes or integrated data flows. Regardless of operating model, though, senior management must focus primarily on business process changes. Systems changes simply support what will be significant business process—and cultural—changes.

Twenty-seven percent of firms are in stage 3. Sometime during stage 3, firms find that IT spending starts to inch back up as they introduce major new systems and become more IT dependent. Stage 3 firms have, on average, IT operating budgets about 10 percent higher than that of stage 2 firms, although still lower than that of stage 1 firms.

Stage 3 benefits. The essence of the optimizing stage is to get the basic business operations digitized. Some firms implement large packaged systems, such as SAP's or Oracle's enterprise resource planning systems. Others rely on major customer relationship management systems. Still others adopt commercial online platforms such as Salesforce.com. Firms with sophisticated IT capabilities build their own platforms. Southwest Airlines, for example, is building its reservation system. And Swiss Re built the process and data access capabilities that make up its platform.

Software is just one piece of the digitized process platform, however. A much tougher piece is the implementation of enterprise processes. The objective is world-class and predictable business processes. Getting business process basics right is not glamorous, but it is essential. For example, one senior executive said his consumer products company had always assumed its value proposition was in rapid introduction of new products. But the firm's large customers started making demands for higher service levels. Initially, the firm was reluctant to invest in reinventing core systems and processes. On further consideration, he said, he felt the firm had no choice: "So what [our key customers] want us to do is to give them an invoice that reflects the items that are on the pallet that we're delivering to them for the price we agreed to charge them." As the senior vice president noted, this really shouldn't be too much to ask.

Of course, in complex organizations, getting the basics right—consistently—*is* a challenge. Arguably, Southwest Airlines' remarkable feat of thirty-five consecutive profitable years was the result of the firm's consistency in getting the basics right. But as the firm became more complex, management recognized a need to rely on IT to sustain and improve operations. As CEO

Gary Kelly noted, getting the basics of its core processes and systems right meant that senior management had to accept some fundamental principles regarding IT: "We all had to agree that we were going to have one platform instead of ten. We needed one version of the truth, not multiple databases full of fares, multiple copies of the schedule, multiple this, multiple that."[6]

Well-managed stage 3 firms can document operational savings. At the global food giant Nestlé, for example, a critical management objective of its global business optimization project (called GLOBE) was to bring down selling, general, and administrative costs to increase earnings before interest and taxes (EBIT). Over the seven years that Nestlé has been implementing standardized and integrated processes, EBIT has increased from 12 to 14 percent. In 2007 alone, that meant almost $2 billion on the bottom line. Chairman and CEO Peter Brabeck-Letmathe attributed Nestlé's performance improvement to the firm's GLOBE project.[7]

Transitioning from stage 3 to stage 4. The strategic objective of the optimizing stage is business operational efficiency. Invariably, optimizing involves reduced business process autonomy for middle managers. Thus, it can be a tough sell. New incentives are usually critical to adoption, but the result is a powerful digitized platform that provides a stable foundation for business operations. Here are characteristics signaling that the firm has achieved the objectives of stage 3 and is positioned for stage 4:

- Business operating costs are decreasing as a percentage of revenues.

- The core transactions of the firm are standardized, digitized, and streamlined as appropriate for the firm's operating model.

- Each core business process has a senior executive owner accountable for continuous improvement and performance outcomes.

- Customer service is world-class and predictable.

- IT spending is increasing as a percentage of the firm's total expense budget, but unit IT costs are stable or decreasing.

- Management establishes project priorities based on strategic enterprise requirements, rather than isolated ROI estimates.

- But . . . the focus on standardizing and integrating has left little management bandwidth for innovating.

Stage 4: Reusing

In the fourth stage, management channels the potential of the firm's digitized process platform by empowering employees to innovate. Managers develop modules leveraging the platform. The modules allow local customization to the platforms of process-oriented firms and enable product line expansion for data-oriented firms such as financial and IT services.

Stage 4 benefits. Only 2 percent of the firms we've studied have reached stage 4, so we are only beginning to understand all the opportunities available to well-managed firms with a powerful digitized process platform. Some early initiatives, however, have started to demonstrate the potential benefits of platform reuse. Pioneers in stage 4 spent generously and confidently, with average IT budgets 45 percent higher than stage 1 firms.[8]

eBay, the $8 billion online marketplace, has a reusable (and heavily reused) digitized platform for online auctions. That platform includes finely tuned digitized processes to list an item for auction, to manage bidding, to manage payments, and to collect and share reputational information about participants. eBay's online auction platform is a stage 4 platform offering constant opportunities for innovation.[9] Former CIO Brad Peterson explains: "The common platform was the innovation that allowed eBay to take off, that was the ability to trade with people all around the world across languages, across boundaries . . . It's a platform that is constantly being added to."

EBay regularly leverages its platform with incremental innovations—for example, it has created a notification system that alerts bidders in an eBay auction whether their bids have been surpassed. Another innovation includes an automated bidding feature that responds to competitive bids within preset limits. The bidder can then leave the eBay site, and the automated feature takes over. The core platform supports online auctions in most—but not all—of the twenty-five countries in which eBay is based.

Internationally, eBay is more like a stage 1 firm as it rapidly adds new geographies and products that are both home grown and acquired. At a future date, eBay may choose a more unified firmwide operating model and build a firmwide digitized platform to support it. This combination of a stage 4 auction platform in the United States and stage 1 platform internationally has helped eBay become one of the fastest growing and most highly valued companies in its first ten years of operation.

Stage 4 firms can also leverage their digitized platforms when they acquire new firms. Firms like Cisco can rip out and replace much of the core infrastructure, processes, and systems in the firms they acquire.[10] They can then install their own core platform. Finally, like Amazon, a few firms have prospered by selling their platforms so that they can generate revenues from other firms' reuse. Amazon Web Services provides Amazon's developer customers with access to centrally provided infrastructure services based on Amazon's own technology platform. Services include Amazon Elastic Compute Cloud, Amazon Simple Storage Service, and Amazon Flexible Payments Service.[11]

Settling into stage 4. To benefit from reusing their digitized platforms, firms must learn how to quickly identify the strategic opportunities that leverage their platform. Senior management ensures that these innovations enhance the firm's performance by providing a clear vision and operating model. This vision establishes both performance objectives to guide local innovations and strategic objectives to guide the nature of the opportunities the firm pursues. You'll know you've reached stage 4 when you observe the following characteristics about your firm's business processes and IT:

- Local managers buy and build innovative business modules that use the firm's existing digitized platform.

- Empowered local decision makers leverage the power of transparent data to address daily customer needs in the context of firmwide performance objectives.

- IT spending increases but includes some outsourced business processes.

- IT unit costs are low compared with other firms.

- The digitized process platform facilitates transparent data flow with external business partners.

- IT-savvy senior managers design the firm's governance to encourage both local innovation and firmwide platform enhancement.

THE MULTIPLE JOURNEYS OF COMPLEX FIRMS

In chapter 2 we observed that large, complex firms have operating models at multiple levels. These firms need to build platforms for each of their operating models. Thus, they will embark on multiple journeys. It is not unusual for different parts of a firm to find themselves at different stages of the IT savvy journey.

For example, the U.S. business of PepsiAmericas, the bottling company, has built a stage 3 platform. That platform has endeared PepsiAmericas to its powerful customers. But in recent years the firm has expanded into eastern Europe to take advantage of the much larger growth opportunities in that market. PepsiAmericas is only slowly instituting the disciplined systems and processes from its U.S. business in its fast-growing eastern European businesses. Management does not want its stable U.S. processes to hinder development of new and different processes that could define an emerging market.[12]

By not prematurely forcing those processes into the less mature growth market, PepsiAmericas has been able to quickly experiment with new business models in eastern Europe, taking advantage of the agility that comes from being small and new. The U.S. business, being more established and considerably bigger, achieves more of its agility from reuse of disciplined processes. This does not mean that PepsiAmericas cannot leverage its learning as it expands. Already, management is identifying opportunities to reuse its approach to building and using centralized data to enhance local decision making.

The process of growing through acquisition challenges a firm's progress on its journey. New acquisitions invariably introduce new variability into the firm's technology platform as well as new processes and systems. If the firm intends to operate with a diversification operating model, the acquisition has less impact on the firm's digitized platform—and vice versa.

Other operating models, however, demand integration and standardization efforts, which can stall progress on the IT savvy journey. Savvy firms such as Cisco and CEMEX take advantage of their established platforms to rip out the acquired firm's technologies, systems, and processes and implement the parent firm's platform. Even with a solid platform, integration is a major effort, but the platform is a valuable asset accelerating realization of postmerger synergies.

LEADING THE CHANGE

The four stages are a reminder that building a digitized platform is a journey. Along that journey, firms learn how to rethink their strategies for a digital economy, how to invest in IT to build digital capabilities, how to design and implement disciplined transaction processes, and how to innovate to leverage their distinctive capabilities.

The IT savvy journey demands extraordinary leaders—leaders who can envision operational strategies for a digital economy and then channel organizational energies to achieve them. Figure 4-2 highlights the "feeling" of that journey. From the enterprise perspective, the IT savvy journey

FIGURE 4-2

Global and local views of the IT savvy journey

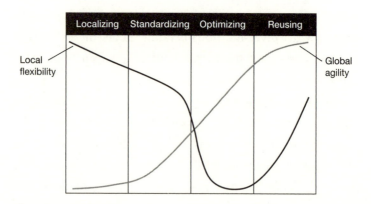

Source: J. Ross, P. Weill, and D. Robertson, *Enterprise Architecture as Strategy: Creating a Foundation for Business Execution* (Boston: Harvard Business School Press, 2006).

leads to increasing global agility. From the local manager's perspective, however, the journey can seem downhill. In the first stage, local managers define system requirements, shell out the money to buy what they want, and generally get what they ask for. That local autonomy diminishes as the firm identifies enterprise synergies. In the third stage, local managers may feel like their hands are tied when new global systems and processes are introduced—particularly if the firm implements a large purchased package system. Finally, in the fourth stage, as they learn to leverage global capabilities, local managers start to recognize the benefits of *not* having to concern themselves with the design of common business processes and data.

Getting to that point of acceptance and implanting the discipline required to build and leverage a digitized platform is a huge leadership challenge. Whether a firm succeeds in building and benefiting from a digitized platform depends, to a large extent, on how well leaders guide their firms through what often involves both cultural and political upheaval. Everything you've ever learned about leadership will be important to pulling this off, but one leadership tool will be particularly important to the success of your IT savvy journey—IT governance. That's the topic of the next chapter.

Allocating Decision Rights and Accountability

Around 2000, when UPS was moving aggressively into eastern Europe, UPS's regional head proposed equipping drivers and warehouses with technology different from UPS's standard handheld device. He could demonstrate that in eastern Europe the nonstandard approach would cost less and be adequate to meet the needs of a less mature market. Then, as now, UPS had an IT decision-making process that reviewed exceptions to these types of standards. In this case, the decision was passed up to senior management, who insisted that eastern Europe adopt standard UPS business processes and technology. Then UPS CEO Mike Eskew explained: "We are a network and we can't have some warehouses managing with this system and others managing with that system . . . [When you allow differences] you can't transfer people and you can't transfer information."[1]

UPS was building out a digitized platform providing global visibility into data and standard core processes to meet the needs of its unification operating model. Management was determined to extend that platform and generate benefits. Because of management's commitment to the digitized platform, whenever UPS changes the functionality of its handheld devices or the systems with which the devices interact, management knows that all parts of the network will still be compatible. UPS has achieved this desired predictability because management has implemented decision-making practices to build, protect, and leverage its digitized platform.

Not every firm needs as much process integration and standardization as UPS's package delivery business. But every firm, at some level, needs a digitized platform to operate effectively. The only way to deliver a digitized platform—and superior business value from IT—is to design IT decision rights and accountabilities so that daily decisions about IT support the firm's strategic goals. Otherwise, IT is destined to become an obstacle to long-term success.

We refer to a firm's framework of IT decision rights and accountabilities as *IT governance*. For some people, the term *governance* conjures up visions of bureaucracy or endless committee meetings. We see the opposite. Governance empowers people by providing transparency about decision-making processes and criteria. Effective IT governance minimizes bureaucracy and dysfunctional politics—and it pays off.

Firms with above-average IT governance effectiveness had 20 percent higher profits as measured by three-year industry-adjusted return on assets (ROA).[2]

FIVE KEY DECISIONS

To effectively govern IT, firms must allocate decision rights and accountabilities for at least five decisions:

- *IT principles:* As explained in chapter 2, strategic use of IT requires that management specify the firm's operating model. *IT principles* refer to the firm's operating model and any other directives clarifying the role of IT in the firm. Governance should allocate decision rights for determining IT principles—usually to one or more members of the senior management team.

- *Enterprise architecture:* Enterprise architecture refers to the design of the firm's digitized platform. Governance should specify the people responsible for establishing business process, data, and technology standards and for dealing with requests for exceptions to those standards.

- *IT infrastructure:* Infrastructure is the set of shared IT services available to all parts of the enterprise. Governance allocates responsibility for defining, providing, and pricing IT shared services.

- *Business needs and project deliverables:* New systems and processes emerge from an extended organizational effort that starts with a business case for a new system and ends, ideally, with a review of the outcomes of that system implementation. Governance allocates ownership for defining the business case, ensuring successful implementation, and delivering the benefits.

- *IT investment and prioritization:* In chapter 3, we discussed the IT funding and prioritization process in depth. Although critical, IT investment and prioritization is only one of five IT decisions that needs to be governed. Here we discuss how it fits with the other four governance decisions.

Firms implement governance through a set of mechanisms: individual roles (e.g., CEO or CIO), committees or teams (e.g., IT steering committee or IT leadership team), and formalized processes (e.g., architecture exception processes or business case review processes). A firm's governance mechanisms clarify how each of the five decisions will be made and who will be held accountable. Southwest Airlines offers an example of how an IT-savvy firm designs IT governance to fulfill strategic business objectives.

IT GOVERNANCE AT SOUTHWEST AIRLINES

Southwest Airlines is a $9.5 billion U.S. airline offering primarily short-haul, point-to-point, low-fare flights. Founded in 1971, Southwest built locally optimal systems until the late 1990s, when CFO Gary Kelly started pushing the use of IT to enhance operational efficiencies and customer service.

When Kelly became CEO in 2004, he worked with CIO Tom Nealon to provide a solid platform of digitized processes for the enterprise.

Although business leaders agreed that enterprise systems and processes would be valuable, they struggled to define those processes. To support enterprise thinking, Southwest created seven strategy teams. These strategy teams, with names like Low-Cost Carrier, Best Place to Work, and Best Customer Experience, meet twice a month to define enterprise priorities for implementing the strategy. The top thirty leaders of the company each sit on two or more strategy teams so they can inform their colleagues of services and needs within their own functional area while learning about the operations of other functional areas. The teams propose enterprise IT projects, which are reviewed by the firm's executive committee in establishing project priorities. Around 80 percent of Southwest's technology projects are aligned with one of the strategy teams.

To ensure that individual projects deliver on their business objectives, Southwest has implemented a tollgate process. The tollgates are monthly reviews of each project's progress and objectives. The tollgates bring together IT and non-IT people who are responsible for resolving any technology and business issues that could hinder project delivery or business value.

One of the tollgates involves a review of the technology that the project team proposes to use to support the new system. In the review process, a group of IT professionals, known as the architecture working group, works with application developers and business people to make sure proposed technologies are either architecturally compliant or the project justifies an exception to standards.

Table 5-1 provides a high-level chart of Southwest's accountability framework for its five governance decisions. Southwest has specified one person or group of persons ultimately accountable for each decision, but the governance design also assigns some specific decisions to other individuals or teams within a decision area. Overlapping participation on decision-making bodies helps to coordinate the five IT decisions to provide consistency in the firm's strategic pursuits.

Management's commitment to building a digitized platform in support of customer service and operational efficiency has made Southwest the United States' largest (in terms of passengers flown) and most profitable airline. In October 2008, while most U.S. airlines were reporting losses, Southwest reported its seventieth consecutive quarterly operating profit.

IT GOVERNANCE OBJECTIVES

Southwest's governance fulfills two critical IT governance objectives: (1) promote desirable behavior in the management and use of IT, and (2) formalize organizational learning about IT and digitized processes. When governance achieves these objectives, firms make consistent progress on their IT savvy journey and IT becomes a strategic asset.

Promote Desirable Behavior in the Management and Use of IT

We tend to assume that we can motivate desirable behavior through appropriate organizational structures and incentive

TABLE 5-1

Southwest Airlines' governance

| Accountable party | **DECISION** | | | | |
	IT principles	Enterprise architecture	IT infrastructure strategies	Business need and project deliverables	IT investment
CEO	Accountable				
CIO		Accountable for technology standards	Accountable	Leads tollgate reviews	
Executive committee[a]					Accountable for enterprise priorities
Strategy teams[b]		Accountable for process and data standards			Accountable for team's priorities
Business leaders				Accountable	
Architecture working group[c]		Conducts compliance reviews			

Source: Researcher interpretation of Southwest's governance design.

a. includes CEO and CIO
b. includes business leaders
c. reports to CIO

systems. But in most firms that's not enough. Enterprisewide objectives are often in conflict with subunit objectives. Individuals don't always understand how their behavior affects firmwide performance. They focus on the local objectives they understand and can achieve. One role of IT governance mechanisms is to encourage desirable behaviors that organizational structures and incentive systems cannot or do not motivate.

For example, an architecture review process aligns individual projects with the enterprise's objectives for a digitized platform. That way, individuals need not fully comprehend how their individual initiatives affect enterprise objectives. The governance process reconciles the local initiative with the enterprise's long-term plan. Of course, management doesn't want an IT group to force compliance with a standard if an exception can introduce valuable change to the firm. Thus, architecture working groups like Southwest's and UPS's usually escalate to senior managers the few exception decisions that they believe could have long-term strategic implications.

Governance should surface and institutionalize natural tensions. Take, for example, the pressure IT professionals feel to ensure the reliability and security of the firm's technology environment. How can they minimize downtime and security breaches? Limit access; take no risks; avoid change. Business leaders, on the other hand, feel constant pressure to seize strategic opportunities and build efficiencies. How do they do that? Experiment; demand data access for themselves and their customers; rapidly implement new system capabilities. The goals of these two groups are both potentially value-adding, but they will often be in conflict. A set of governance mechanisms, such as senior management strategy committees, disciplined project methodologies, and architecture reviews, exposes and helps resolve these valuable tensions to the benefit of the enterprise.

Formalize Organizational Learning About IT and Digitized Processes

Governance should help firms learn so that they stop making the same mistakes over and over again. Southwest's tollgate process engages stakeholders in system delivery and implementation. This not only improves outcomes on the current project, but also gives them valuable experience in recognizing what goes right and wrong in delivering projects. This learning from experience is the essence of what makes a firm IT savvy.

Post-implementation reviews (PIR) support organizational learning. PIRs help management recognize when their expectations for the benefits and costs of a new system are realized—and when those expectations were unrealistic. PIRs are valuable when they foster learning—they are not a useful governance mechanism when they simply assign blame for failures. By involving key stakeholders over the entire life cycle of development, implementation, and post-implementation review, a project methodology with intermittent reviews keeps a project on track for timely delivery and significant business benefits.

An architecture review process also supports learning. Architecture reviews help an organization learn how to effectively use standard technologies to meet business needs. Just as important, the review process identifies when standards are outdated or no longer adequate for addressing the business needs of the firm.

IT governance should always encourage desirable behavior and formalize organizational learning about IT and digitized processes. However, there is no single optimal governance design. As firms move through the four stages of the IT savvy journey, their governance objectives—and thus their governance design—evolve. In particular, a business transformation imposes unique requirements for IT governance.

IT GOVERNANCE FOR BUSINESS TRANSFORMATION

Chapter 4 described the four stages of the IT savvy journey. When a firm enters the third stage, it attempts to build a digitized platform. The data and process standards that firms implement in this stage fundamentally transform their operations. A business transformation requires governance designed to lead change and clarify new business processes and expectations. Campbell Soup Company illustrates how well-designed project-level governance guides a firm through the transformation from locally optimized business processes to enterprise thinking.

Governance at Campbell Soup Company

Founded in 1869, Campbell Soup Company is an $8 billion global manufacturer of soups, baked snacks, beverages, and chocolates.[3] In May 2004, following a successful three-year effort to develop a solid IT infrastructure, Campbell embarked on a $125 million, three-year project to implement an ERP and introduce common processes and shared data across Campbell's twenty-two North American businesses.

Dubbed Project Harmony, Campbell's transformation effort focused on standardizing three core business processes across the firm: make-to-ship, account-to-report, and order-to-cash. By standardizing and integrating these three processes, Campbell created a global supply chain and reduced operating costs. Management articulated project goals in terms of total delivered cost (TDC), the total cost of making product and delivering it to customers. Employees throughout the firm were charged with flat TDC, meaning that annual costs would stay the same regardless of inflation.

Management recognized two major challenges associated with the transformation project: (1) process design—Campbell wanted to optimize its three core processes while meeting the individual needs of the twenty-two businesses—and (2) process adoption—Campbell's people would need to learn new behaviors supporting an enterprise, rather than local, view of business success. To address these two challenges, management created new roles and accountabilities.

At the highest level, four senior executives took responsibility for IT principles: the CIO, the CFO, the president of Campbell North America, and senior vice president for global supply chain. At their biweekly meetings, these executives reviewed progress and provided resources to ensure that Project Harmony met targets. All requests for deviations from standard had to pass through this team, which severely limited the number of exception requests. The sponsor team also identified projects to put on hold to maintain focus on Project Harmony implementation.

At the next level, an experienced IT executive was named project leader. He headed the operating committee, which included a technical lead, an IBM project lead, Campbell's leader for change management, and three experienced senior managers, each of whom led one of the three process teams. The operating committee met weekly to make decisions on the interdependencies among the process areas as well as to ensure that the overall program remained on track.

The project team comprised sixty Campbell people and seventy consultants also reported to the project leader. The project team was charged with implementing the system. Three process advisory groups advised the process teams. The advisory groups were chaired by senior executives.

Finally, deployment teams in each of the twenty-two businesses were responsible for timely implementation and change management at the individual sites. Recognizing the magnitude of the changes and heavy resource requirements, the deployment teams staged or killed most other change initiatives, including product rollouts, pricing changes, and new promotion efforts.

The sponsor team and operating committee worked with deployment teams to enable learning across the twenty-two locations. As each site implemented Project Harmony, the deployment team from the next site was on hand to learn critical success factors and potential stumbling blocks. Meanwhile, senior leadership emphasized that the goal of every manager was not just the success of the current implementation but also the success of the next one.

Campbell management designed the chart shown in figure 5-1 to clarify decision-making rights and accountability for Project Harmony. These decision makers led Project

Harmony to an on-time and on-budget completion and exceeded business performance expectations. In 2007 Campbell generated shareholder returns of 16.2 percent, compared with an average of 7.7 percent earned by S&P's packaged food index.

Project Harmony's success was due, in part, to the centralization of accountability in the four-person executive team. These executives held themselves accountable for articulating project principles, establishing the high-level enterprise architecture, delivering project benefits, and deciding on implementation priorities. But they also implemented governance mechanisms for coordinating the decisions of everyone involved with Project Harmony. The efforts of all the teams and working groups contributed to achieving project objectives. That coordination is a particular challenge in IT governance.

USING MECHANISMS TO BRIDGE STAKEHOLDER PERSPECTIVES

While IT governance necessarily assigns strategic decisions to senior executives, governance must also ensure that IT decisions made at the top of the firm are consistently applied by decision makers at lower levels of the firm. Six stakeholder groups make decisions affecting how IT is managed and used. These six groups, shown in the shaded rectangles in figure 5-2, are the IT and business leaders at the enterprise, business unit, and project levels.

To help you establish, review, or rationalize your IT governance, consider the following five IT governance mechanisms. These mechanisms are used by top-performing firms

FIGURE 5-1

Project Harmony decision-making rights

	Project mgmt	Basic design and process/control changes within process area or workstream	Major process/control changes within process area	Cross-process/cross workstream	Deployment decisions	Business unit organization and policy changes	Company organization and policy changes	Scope/budget change
Sponsor group	Notify		Notify	**Decide**[a]	Notify/**Decide**[b]	Notify	**Decide**[c]	**Decide**[d]
Process advisory group	Notify	Notify	**Decide**	Consult	Notify	Notify	Notify	Consult (scope)
Operating committee	Consult		Notify	Notify	Consult	Notify	Consult	Consult
Program management office (PMO)	Identify/recommend/**Decide**	Notify	Consult	Identify	Recommend		Recommend	Recommend

Project team (process area teams)	Identify/ recommend/ decide	Identify/ recommend	Identify/ recommend/ decide[a]	Identify	Recommend	Identify	Identify
Business deployment team	Notify	Notify	Notify	**Decide**[b]	**Decide**	Consult	Notify

Source: Campbell Soup Company.

a. Basic cross-process decisions will be resolved through cross-process teams as assigned by PMO; major cross-process decisions with alternate viewpoints will be resolved by the sponsor group.

b. Sponsor group decides issues affecting overall deployment approach and schedule; each deployment site makes master planning decisions related to business activities and deployment/cutover activities within the overall schedule and project requirements.

c. May require approval of CEO for major organization or policy changes.

d. Major scope or budget changes may require approval from the board of directors.

FIGURE 5-2

Effective IT governance mechanisms

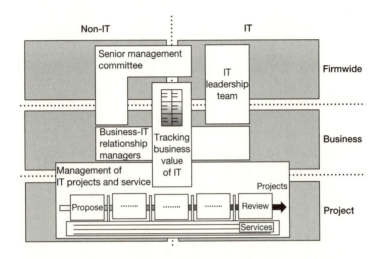

Source: © 2009 MIT Sloan Center for Information Systems Research. Used with permission.

Note: Firms without these IT governance mechanisms had lower IT governance performance (which is significantly correlated to several multiyear measures of firm performance, such as return on equity).

to coordinate the decisions of the six stakeholder groups. Our research has found that firms without these IT mechanisms have worse governance and business performance.[4]

- *Senior management committee:* Not surprisingly, IT-savvy firms consistently engage senior executives in IT decision making. A senior-level committee is often responsible for IT principles and overall IT spending and prioritization. The composition of the senior management IT steering committee usually includes some or all of the firm's top executives, including the CEO, COO, CIO, CFO, and business unit heads. These senior executives can bridge organizational entities, such as business units and functions. Most of the firms we describe in this book have this type of committee, including EMC, BT, Southwest Airlines, State Street Corporation, and UPS.

- *IT leadership team:* Large firms usually invest substantial IT decision-making responsibilities in the IT leadership team. Chaired by the CIO, this team is composed of either the CIO's direct reports, or, in more diversified organizations, the IT heads of the business units and shared services. These executives are often involved in decisions related to enterprise standards, IT infrastructure, and shared services.

- *Business-IT relationship managers:* Large firms generally have relationship managers responsible for linking business and IT. These people act as liaisons to ensure that business users benefit from firmwide IT services while also representing the needs of the business in other IT decisions. Most of the IT-savvy firms described in this book have business IT relationship managers or similar roles. Their efforts typically engage individuals a level below the senior management team and thus support effective implementation of decisions related to business process design, standards compliance, business case development, reuse of systems and data from other parts of the firm, and the tracking of IT value.

- *Management/oversight of IT projects and service:*
  The difference between hoping that a project is delivered on time, on scope, and on budget and actual
  value realization is typically a matter of disciplined
  project methodology and oversight. Responsibility
  for designing project methodology and oversight
  often rests with a project management office (PMO).
  Effective implementation depends on stakeholders
  at all levels of the firm.

  Management and oversight of IT services is equally
  important, because in most firms, IT services account
  for about twice the budget of new IT projects. The key
  IT services provided across the firm must be specified
  and managed for unit cost and quality—part of the IT
  infrastructure and architecture decisions. For example,
  Intel produces a catalogue of IT services and their unit
  costs. Each year Intel benchmarks its IT unit cost and
  quality with a peer group of companies. The results
  are reported in the IT department's annual report,
  published on the Web. This transparency helps
  demonstrate how IT adds value every year and helps
  fine-tune how the services are managed and archi-
  tected together into a platform. Managing IT services
  also involves planning for future needs. This requires
  that the IT unit assess demand against capacity for
  each service.

- *Tracking business value of IT:* Post-implementation
  reviews (PIRs), which provide a formal process for

tracking the value of IT, are particularly valuable for increasing organizational learning about how to generate value from IT. Some firms, such as BT, have moved to midproject reviews every ninety days. To increase accountability, every ninety days each program undergoes a review against the objectives and metrics determined in the plan. If the program does not meet these objectives and metrics, it will typically be cancelled by BT's finance team. To make sure incentives are aligned, bonuses are paid to the teams based in part on the project's ninety-day review of performance against plan.

Figure 5-2 maps how these five mechanisms help bridge the six key stakeholders. Map your key governance mechanisms to assess how well you are driving consistent IT decisions and values involving your six stakeholders. If you detect any gaps, you can bet that IT is not generating the strategic value you want.

Most IT and business executives tell us they are not satisfied with their IT governance. That's understandable. We've already noted that you need to design IT governance mechanisms to address five key decisions, and those governance mechanisms need to coordinate the six stakeholders who make IT decisions. There's more! You need to regularly review your governance practices to make sure they adapt to business changes, particularly increased diversification or globalization. Your governance should reflect your firm's IT maturity on your IT-savvy journey. State Street Corporation provides an instructive example of how to mature and globalize IT governance.

GLOBAL IT GOVERNANCE AT STATE STREET CORPORATION

State Street is a leading provider of financial services to institutional investors, including investment servicing, investment management, and investment research and trading. State Street's customers—asset managers, hedge funds, insurance companies, collective funds, mutual funds, pension funds, and nonprofit institutions including endowments and foundations—use State Street services to deliver value to their clients, control costs, launch new products, and expand globally. State Street's more than twenty-eight thousand employees work in twenty-six countries serving customers in over one hundred markets. The firm's 2007 revenues of $8.4 billion represented an annual increase of 17 percent per year for five years with 18 percent annual increases in earnings per share. As of December 31, 2007, State Street had $15.3 trillion in assets under custody.[5]

State Street's products and services are highly IT-enabled, so the firm has typically allocated 20 percent of operating expenses to IT. Historically, State Street had been a set of autonomous business units (e.g., investment management, pension funds), each focused on developing value for their customers. When David Spina became chairman and CEO of State Street in 2001, he faced a slumping market and a changing industry. To increase customer service while wringing greater value from the firm's assets, he articulated a new strategy of "One State Street."

State Street revamped IT structure and governance to enable its new strategy. At the highest level, State Street created, the IT executive committee (ITEC), comprising the COO, the CAO, the CIO, and senior executives from State Street's various business units. ITEC established the IT principles supporting the firm's operating model and prioritized the enterprisewide IT budget accordingly. ITEC considered the firm's strategic objectives and monitored the resources and progress of the projects through an enterprise-wide IT budget and activity tracking system.

To define an IT strategy that delivered the requirements of both the business units and the enterprise, the CIO's staff consisted of twelve direct reports, half of whom headed up enterprise services, while the other half were responsible for business unit relationships. Enterprise services were delivered according to carefully designed service-level agreements and chargeback. The service-level agreements forced decision makers at multiple levels to surface and resolve the natural tensions between enterprise services and business unit demands. The CIO also created an IT leadership group of all IT senior vice presidents. This group met regularly to identify enterprise synergies and to implement IT strategy. An Office of Architecture within IT took on responsibility for implementing standards and monitoring architecture compliance.

These mechanisms, which State Street implemented in 2002, promoted learning and helped the firm adopt the "One State Street" strategy. Figure 5-3 describes how these mechanisms coordinated the six key stakeholders' perspectives.[6] As State Street has become increasingly IT savvy, however, the firm has fine-tuned its governance mechanisms. For example, the firm outgrew the need for ITEC as a stand-alone committee to

FIGURE 5-3

IT governance at State Street

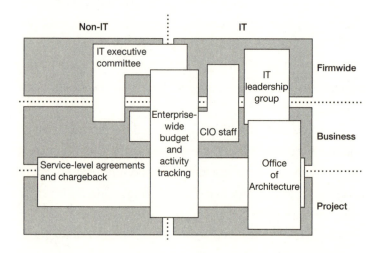

Source: © 2009 MIT Sloan Center for Information Systems Research. Used with permission.

Note: Diagram is based on the IT engagement model framework developed by Nils Fonstad (INSEAD). State Street data is the authors' interpretation.

deal with IT issues. In 2006 ITEC was disbanded. Instead, former CIO Joseph Antonellis championed IT issues at meetings of the Executive Operating Group, a small group of senior executives headed by CEO Ron Logue.

In 2008, Joe Antonellis became State Street's vice chairman. The new CIO, Chris Perretta, is leading IT governance refinements to focus on global issues and business process optimization. State Street's governance is being fine-tuned to incorporate its increasingly distributed operations, which include business process servicing in India and new-product development in China. Perretta is restructuring IT into three building blocks: corporate (e.g., IT leadership, IT portfolio management, and IT security), shared services (e.g., strategic sourcing, offshore services, data services, and infrastructure), and business-aligned services (e.g., new initiatives, business IT relationship management, and client integration). He is designing decision rights and accountability for each building block to achieve a balance between local business innovation and global economies of scale.

In the next stage of the firm's IT savvy journey, executive vice president Robert Kaplan is leading a new breakthrough effort called Model Office. His multifunctional team is identifying and standardizing the core set of global business processes at State Street. This effort will require creation of twenty virtual Centers of Excellence, each responsible for the delivery of critical business processes (e.g., trade processing), which will be optimized across several geographical centers servicing all of State Street's global operations. These new governance mechanisms will help State Street coordinate decision making in an increasingly global business. New governance mechanisms usually take time to master, but they are essential to a firm's ability to promote desirable behavior and facilitate ongoing learning.

CREATING TRANSPARENT IT GOVERNANCE

For effective IT governance, you and your colleagues must all understand how the key IT decisions in your firm should be made. Think about the way financial decisions are made in your firm. The decision rights and accountabilities (i.e., governance) for financial decisions specify how you and your colleagues make a capital investment, who sets the budget, who is responsible for business profitability, what gets audited, and so on. What percentage of your firm's senior managers could accurately describe the way key financial decisions are made? Ninety-five percent? Higher? It's hard to imagine doing business without everybody understanding how key financial decisions are made and how people are held accountable.

What percentage of your senior management colleagues could describe how key IT decisions are made and how people are held accountable? In our research, the average answer is 45 percent.[7] For many firms, particularly less IT-intensive and small to medium-sized firms, the number is 25 percent or lower. This is an important metric because the higher that percentage, the more bottom line impact we see from IT—in fact, it's one of the best indicators of IT value that we have.[8]

To conclude, here are five important principles from our research to guide your IT governance work:

- *Lead the effort to set or clarify your operating model:* Your operating model specifies which decisions will be global and which will be local. By making the operating model—and accompanying desirable behavior—clear, you as a senior executive can delegate many IT decisions.

- *For transparency, draw up IT governance on one page and use it to communicate decision-making accountability:* Map your IT governance mechanisms and the individuals responsible for them using one of the figures in this chapter. Make it your goal to get the percentage of senior executives who understand how IT decisions are made to 95 percent.

- *Keep the number of governance mechanisms small:* Some firms introduce a new mechanism in response to every problem. The result is uncoordinated—and ineffective and confusing—IT governance. Assign someone (typically the CIO) the responsibility for designing and implementing a coherent set of IT governance mechanisms.

- *Play to your strengths:* Rebecca Rhoads, global CIO of Raytheon, advises implementing IT governance that overlays "whatever makes your company great."[9] Wherever possible, overlay IT decisions onto strong governance mechanisms used for other assets (e.g., operating committee, capital expenditure process, business process teams, project management office) rather than establishing IT-specific mechanisms. You will need some IT-specific mechanisms, but keep those to a minimum (e.g., IT leadership team, business-IT relationship managers, and management of IT projects and services).

- *Learn from exceptions:* If there is a good reason for an exception, such as building a new system that doesn't use the firm's current technology standards, grant it and learn from it. Make the exceptions process fast and easy, and make it require political capital so it's not used frivolously.

By clarifying IT decision rights and accountability, you create the management capability to progress along the IT savvy journey. In the next chapter, we'll describe the opportunities you'll create as you become more IT savvy.

6

Driving Value from IT

Your team has now created and integrated a platform of strategy, players, facilities, marketing, scouting, and training to profit and grow. You are now ready to become a champion team. What's left?

Surprisingly, firms sometimes push themselves through transformations and then fail to reap the benefits. Exhausted from the effort of putting in new systems and processes, they revert to old behaviors. Once you've put in a digitized platform, you need to actively drive value from it. The firms that are best at this start driving value early. If you start driving value from a platform even as you take the first small steps toward building it, you will reduce the disruptions of major transformations. That's the goal. Build a little, benefit a lot; build some more, benefit some more; and so on.

This chapter discusses how to drive benefits from your digitized platform. We start with 7-Eleven Japan (SEJ), a firm that's been driving value from a digitized platform for over twenty years. SEJ demonstrates how IT-savvy firms develop a pattern of building and enhancing a platform to drive sustained business benefits.[1]

DELIVERING VALUE FROM A DIGITIZED PLATFORM AT 7-ELEVEN JAPAN

7-Eleven Japan's CEO, Toshifumi Suzuki, has long believed that one of the most serious problems in retail is a missed sale because of an out-of-stock item. Accordingly, since he opened his first store in 1974, Suzuki has consistently enhanced his stores' inventory and product management capabilities. Early on, he defined a replication operating model that has, over time, installed world-class technology and distribution management processes into each of SEJ's 12,034 stores. As a result, each store optimizes inventory to meet the demands of its own customers.

How do they do that? SEJ's success stems from skilled in-store employees taking advantage of the capabilities of its digitized platform. SEJ introduced its first point of sale system (POS) in the early 1980s. The data the POS generated helped SEJ analyze its customers' buying habits to improve the product ordering process. The POS data became even more valuable in the early 1990s, when SEJ installed high-speed telecommunications lines and, subsequently, satellite connections. High-speed telecommunications led to instantaneous sales reports to SEJ's entire supply chain, which allowed SEJ to further collapse the time between sale and replenishment.

Since then, SEJ has created a "total information system" to connect its stores, headquarters, and supplier sites. At the stores, employees have access to recent sales, weather conditions, and product range information, all presented graphically to support ordering decisions. To drive maximum value from its platform, SEJ trains all store owners and clerks, including part-time workers, on inventory management. Counselors visit stores twice a week to provide advice on store operations and information on available products.

SEJ management insists on the professional development of all employees. These employees order fresh food for delivery three times a day, so whether or not SEJ achieves optimum product mix depends on their decisions. Daily feedback on store performance helps employees constantly improve their product mix management. Store employees can also work directly with manufacturers to propose new items. Their efforts have resulted in constant product innovation—a remarkable 70 percent of products are new each year in each store.

From a customer's perspective, SEJ's effective use of the platform means that on hot days, 7-Eleven Japan stores have plenty of Bento boxes, whereas on cold days there are lots of hot noodles for sale. SEJ, in turn, benefits from both customer loyalty and higher sales. Over the years, SEJ has consistently outperformed competitors on average daily sales and margin.

As growth opportunities have slowed in Japan, SEJ has pursued other innovations that expand on the firm's core infrastructure and existing store services. In 2001, SEJ established IYBank through a joint venture and installed ATMs in its stores. Subsequent innovations have added services such as the printing of digital pictures (2004), electronic ticket sales (2006), "Otoriyose-bin" Web shopping (2007), and "nanaco" electronic money service (2007).[2] These new services allow SEJ to test the boundaries of its retail and customer service platform.

SEJ is driving value by making sure everyone uses its capabilities and then tirelessly introducing new capabilities. This is a habit you'll want to develop in your firm.

LEVERAGING A DIGITIZED PLATFORM FOR BUSINESS AGILITY

The goal of a digitized platform is profitable growth from business agility and streamlined operations. Historically, firms have gone through cycles of growth followed by profit. But today's global business environment demands simultaneous profit and growth. *Business agility*, which we define as the use of existing process and IT capabilities to rapidly generate new business value while limiting costs and risks, enables profitable growth.

The essence of business agility is reuse. And the purpose of a digitized platform is to create a set of reusable systems and business processes that knowledgeable people can deploy quickly. By facilitating reuse, a platform gives a firm a head start on related business opportunities.

Like at SEJ, your firm's platform can provide business agility. Our research has found that business agility allows a firm to rapidly respond to four types of business opportunities: (1) enhancing performance by empowering people with optimized processes and data, (2) accelerating product and service innovation, (3) better meeting customer needs by reorganizing, and (4) better integrating mergers and acquisitions.[3] Table 6-1 summarizes these opportunities and how you can cash in on them. Let's look at how some IT-savvy firms have driven value from a digitized platform.

TABLE 6-1

How a platform leads to business agility

Business opportunity	Role of the digitized platform	Important management practices
Enhanced performance by empowering people	• Make customer and product/service data available to customer-facing and operational employees • Provide analytics to decision makers	• Employee training • Clear performance objectives and metrics to encourage ownership of objectives • Collaboration with counterparts to share learning
Accelerated product and service innovation	• Automate repetitive processes to allow more management focus on innovation • Facilitate, through standard interfaces, addition of new products and replication across sites • Introduce information-based customer services • Create revenue-generating services	• Incentives rewarding innovation • Functional teams who solicit and evaluate product innovation ideas • Customer relationship managers who seek out customer needs and suggestions • Incubators charged with generating new products and services

TABLE 6-1 *(continued)*

How a platform leads to business agility

Reorganization around customers	• Provide information to support decisions specific to individual customer segments • Provide straight-through processing to support global functions	• New roles specializing in specific customer segments • New structures such as centralized call centers; global functions; shared services
Integration of a merger or acquisition	• Provide a platform to replace systems and processes of acquired firm • Provide process components that can be reused in acquired business	• Rip and replace approach to integration • Selective use of process components

Source: © 2009 MIT Sloan Center for Information Systems Research. Used with permission.

Enhancing Performance by Empowering People

One of the most valuable characteristics of a digitized platform is its ability to put information into the hands of people who need it. Do not miss this opportunity! Every employee who interacts with customers can be armed with information on the customer and the firm's products and services to ensure a quality interaction. But you'll need to make sure they (1) have access to needed information, (2) know how to get it, and (3) know what to do with it.

Campbell Soup employees improve operational processes. Campbell Soup's management insisted that every Campbell's site in North America implement the firm's standard supply chain processes.[4] The standard processes produce standard data, which allows a global view of the supply chain. Leaders of Campbell's Project Harmony provided training on the new system tools, but they knew that they could not generate all the potential benefits of a global supply chain if employees merely learned how to use the new systems.

The next step was to make sure people understood how to drive value from their new systems. To that end, process owners have taken responsibility for circulating good ideas they observe at individual plants. In addition, management encourages employees to collaborate with colleagues at other sites—a practice that builds on relationships formed during the implementation process.

To further encourage learning, management has consistently focused on flat total delivered cost (TDC), the stated goal of Project Harmony. As employees come to understand the components of TDC, they increasingly accept ownership for generating benefits from their new systems. For example, customer care employees have learned how to manage by exception; they follow up on fewer order problems while responding more effectively to orders needing their attention. Supply chain managers have found they can diagnose errors more quickly. These diagnoses lead to additional training when errors result from people's mistakes. Plant managers are claiming significant savings from faster recognition of equipment problems. And a controller found that process improvements reduced the control points for Sarbanes-Oxley compliance efforts from more than sixty to around twenty.[5]

At Campbell, the TDC objective provides a team objective. Swiss Re, like many financial services firms, emphasizes more individual performance outcomes.

Empowerment at Swiss Re relies on individual performance metrics. Swiss Re's goal for its platform is to generate consistent economic value in a volatile industry.[6] Of course, individual underwriters, claims administrators, salespersons, investment managers, and other knowledge workers in Swiss Re's local offices couldn't easily assess the impacts of their individual decisions on Swiss Re's economic value. To ensure that local decisions meet the firm's global objectives, Swiss Re is centralizing responsibility for defining decision criteria and performance targets. Management can then hold individuals accountable for the results of their decisions.

Swiss Re's digitized platform enables management to isolate the returns on various types of investments and contracts. With this information they can analyze performance results and establish criteria for individual decisions. For example, product professionals set target prices for the firm's products (the price estimated to generate Swiss Re's desired return). Customer relationship professionals sell these products to customers using product managers' target prices to make their decisions on what to charge customers.

To reflect their different responsibilities, Swiss Re assesses the performance of product managers based on the accuracy of their target prices. Customer relationship managers are evaluated on how they perform against target prices. The platform's value results, in part, from the transparency it provides for assessing individual performance, even in down times. For employees, the platform provides accurate information to support their decision making, thus making them—and Swiss Re—more successful.

Employee empowerment is not an automatic outcome of a digitized platform. In addition to equipping your employees with valuable information, you must provide ongoing training and clear decision criteria and performance objectives. It's not worth the trouble of building a digitized platform if you're not going to empower your employees with information. Empowerment leads to improved firm performance and a culture of continuous improvement as your people learn how to capitalize on the capabilities of your digitized platform.

Accelerating Innovation on the Platform

You may not normally associate standards with innovation, but the data and process standards introduced with a digitized platform have enhanced innovation at many IT-savvy firms. A platform can support product innovation in a variety of ways. P&G, ING DIRECT, and UPS highlight the different opportunities.

P&G's shared services platform supports brand managers' innovations. At P&G, the shared services platform handles many administrative services that P&G wants to offload from brand managers so that they can focus on innovation and customer responsiveness.[7] In addition, P&G's shared services organization (Global Business Services) delivers reusable business support services, such as prime prospect research, technical package and materials design, competitive intelligence, in-store action planning, and product imaging and modeling. These services leverage firmwide expertise so that brand managers can launch new products quickly and efficiently.

Of course, P&G initially needed to assure brand managers that the design and quality of these services would meet their needs. It's not easy for managers to let go of activities they perform well. P&G's Global Business Services encourages managers with cost savings, while management rewards brand managers for their creative and customer relationship accomplishments.

ING DIRECT's platform supports product innovation. ING DIRECT's platform is the base for its low-cost, high-value personal banking products.[8] The bank's product committee, which has members from each of its country banks, solicits ideas for new products and determines which to pursue. The firm then develops new products centrally, so that all of ING DIRECT's nine country banks can adopt them.

In some cases, local banks may design a financial product to meet the specific needs of their customers. Even then, if management believes a new product or service has wider application across other banks, the central IT unit will develop the product so that it fits the firm's standard interfaces. The firm's platform of standard interfaces reduces the development task, thus speeding new product development and facilitating rapid launch.

UPS's platform supports customer service innovations. UPS uses its platform to provide a constant stream of information-based innovations to serve customers.[9] These started with Web-based services such as tracking, package pickup, and rate checking in the mid-1990s. Over time, services became more customized. UPS started providing information on all of its customers' inbound and outbound packages. It built links to help UPS's customers inform their own customers about packages they had shipped. UPS also offers a dashboard with interactive capabilities for customers who need delivery information for billing or customer service needs.

Most of these innovations are services that provide information about UPS's own package delivery business. But some innovations become revenue generating. UPS's innovations are not simply happy surprises. Management invests in innovation. Account managers work with large customers to identify ways in which UPS can help customers help their customers. And UPS is willing to fund separate innovation teams when it senses new opportunities. UPS positioned itself for digital commerce, for example, by creating a separate incubator team to develop new business ideas.

At a minimum, your digitized platform can perform repetitive processes so that managers have more time to think about innovation. By simply changing expectations to make innovation a part of most managers' jobs, your digitized platform can contribute to your firm's innovativeness. But you can also create teams charged with identifying incremental innovations. In addition, your customers are likely to have plenty of suggestions as to how you can use technology to better serve them. Just ask.

Reorganizing Around Customers

The retailing giant Wal-Mart has established a reputation for offering low prices to customers. Behind the scenes, Wal-Mart has another reputation—for being a very demanding customer of its suppliers. That approach once made Wal-Mart unusual. Increasingly, however, demanding customers have become the norm.

Growing numbers of companies are looking at their organizational structures and sensing that those structures meet their own functional needs better than they meet customer needs. Customers rarely have the patience to work with providers who can't respond to their needs. But many firms do not have the processes or information to organize themselves according to their customers' needs. Now that you have a digitized platform, you can restructure around your customers.

PepsiAmericas reorganizes around customer needs. In 2006, PepsiAmericas' management announced a customer alignment strategy. Like all major bottling companies, PepsiAmericas' go-to-market strategy was built around the trucks that delivered the goods. But PepsiAmericas had thirty national customers responsible for nearly a third of their revenues. In addition, restaurants, which sold fountain drinks, and schools, which sold vending machine drinks, had different needs from large retailers. Management initiated the customer alignment strategy to better leverage existing channel expertise, further specialize in serving customers, allocate resources to growing channels, align with customer processes, and have more visibility into market opportunities.[10]

Customer alignment involved separating out responsibility for large PepsiAmericas' customers who accept shipments at their own warehouses. A second segment consists of large customers who accept direct store delivery. PepsiAmericas also created a call center for smaller accounts, although much of the responsibility for smaller accounts remained in the field. This new structure required very little IT work, because PepsiAmericas' digitized platform had created a data repository for easy access to current and historical data. Data was available to support critical decisions such as pricing and customer service negotiations. Management needed to create new management roles to focus individuals on the needs of specific customer segments, but IT was an enabler, not an obstacle.

Swiss Re reorganizes to meet global requirements. In late 2005, management at Swiss Re sensed that the firm's common processes and systems offered an untapped opportunity to improve customer service and enhance shareholder value. The firm reorganized around three global business functions: client markets, products, and financial services. Management also introduced three corporate functions (risk management, finance, and operations) providing globally coordinated support.

This new structure supported efforts to adopt best-in-class processes in each business function while providing an integrated value chain across businesses. It allowed the firm to manage risk globally and to meet the needs of global customers.[11]

In today's global economy, you need to find a way to meet the growing needs of your customers. Chances are, your current structure isn't delivering. Reorganizations are often traumatic events for the people in a firm. With a digitized platform, you can pick the structure you think is best—not the old one for which your systems were built.

Platform Support for Merger Integration

From an IT perspective, the challenge of growing by acquisition rather than organically is that two companies are invariably trying to merge incompatible systems and processes. Some firms try to pick and choose from the two firms' best capabilities, but the interdependencies of systems and processes complicate the task. Your digitized platform gives you an asset that can add value to the merged entity.

CEMEX grows with a rip and replace strategy. Over the last eight years, Mexico-based CEMEX has grown through acquisitions from a $5 billion USD cement manufacturer to a $22 billion USD global building materials company. CEMEX initiated its acquisition strategy in 1992, when it acquired two Spanish cement producers. Initially, CEMEX added value by introducing best-in-class management practices in the acquired firms. The results were impressive: companies acquired between 1992 and 1996 increased their operating margins by an average of over ten percentage points in the three years after acquisition.[12]

These early acquisitions, however, introduced a proliferation of systems and processes and climbing IT costs. As the firm expanded globally, this became a growing concern, so in 2000, CEO Lorenzo Zambrano introduced a major enterprise resource planning system to help the firm standardize eight key business processes: commercial (customer-facing and cement logistics), ready-mix manufacturing, accounting, planning and budgeting, operations, procurement, finance, and HR. Now each acquisition involves ripping out the acquired firm's systems and processes and implementing CEMEX's platform. The rip and replace experience can be trying for employees at acquired companies, but CEMEX invests heavily in training. The results are remarkable. With operations now in fifty countries, CEMEX grew sales by 19 percent and EBITDA by 11 percent in 2007.

7-Eleven Japan selectively reuses its platform. Some of 7-Eleven Japan's growth in Japan results from acquisitions of stores. Like CEMEX on a smaller scale, SEJ management applied a rip and replace approach to integrating those stores. In 2004, SEJ opened its first store in China. China presents a new opportunity for replicating SEJ's platform.

SEJ's 2005 acquisition of 7-Eleven U.S., however, is not as well suited to a rip and replace strategy. The market share of convenience stores is much lower in the United States, where the market is heterogeneous, the income gap is bigger, and the shopper is more cost sensitive than in Japan. In addition, unlike the Japanese stores that became franchisees one at a time, in the United States, SEJ acquired six thousand stores and franchises all at once. Facing different demographics and an established base of stores, SEJ is not able to simply rip and replace systems and processes. Instead, SEJ can leverage useful elements of its distribution and inventory management processes as it builds a platform for its U.S. business. We expect SEJ will reuse specific business components rather than the entire platform.

A rip and replace strategy is useful only if you are acquiring firms much like your own. If that's what you're doing, the digitized platform is invaluable. Having learned how to implement a platform once, you can apply that learning to the acquired firm. Part of the advantage of reaching stage 4 in the IT savvy journey is that you can identify components for reuse. The ability to reuse process components will be useful for almost any acquisition.

EXPERIMENTING OFF THE PLATFORM

IT-savvy firms drive business agility from their digitized platforms. They empower their people to drive value from their platforms. They introduce product innovations. They reorganize to drive customer value. And they look for opportunities to move into new markets or acquire firms to further leverage their platforms. All of this allows them to grow profitably. But although business agility is necessary for business success, it is not sufficient. Business agility—and the digitized platform enabling it—will not help you respond to disruptive technologies and radically new business models.[13]

The computer manufacturer Dell provides a compelling example of the limitations of a digitized platform. For a number of years, Dell's highly acclaimed business model thrived because the firm had built a distinctive platform supporting individually configured, direct-order personal computers. But Dell's platform didn't help support business success when personal computers essentially became commodities. Although Dell still sells computers, the market opportunities are limited, so the firm is recreating itself as a services provider.[14] Doing so requires building another digitized platform.

You can mitigate the risks of your digitized platform by innovating separately from your platform. This involves explicitly funding business experiments as part of your IT portfolio. UPS offers a case in point.

For many years, UPS could grow by extending its digitized platform that supported package delivery. UPS grew comfortably by moving into new markets and adding innovative package-related services. As growth opportunities in package delivery have slowed, UPS has looked beyond its platform for growth opportunities. Keeping the package delivery business as its core business, UPS has crafted a set of smaller, growth-oriented businesses such as UPS Supply Chain Solutions, UPS Capital, UPS Consulting, UPS Logistics Technologies, The UPS Store, and others.[15]

UPS's invaluable digitized platform doesn't provide much value to the new businesses. In fact, it's quite the opposite. Instead of using the package delivery business's digitized platform to build new businesses, UPS's new businesses feed the core package delivery business. Meanwhile, UPS is building a new digitized platform to support its new businesses.

In designing most strategic experiments outside your core business, you'll want to explicitly avoid using an existing digitized platform. The platform will constrain the vision of what's possible. Separate funding, and often a separate management team, can help identify business innovations that could be instrumental to a firm's long-term success. During intensive platform-building periods, you won't have the bandwidth or the financial resources to invest in experiments. But once the base of a platform is built, look for opportunities to grow beyond your platform.

Don't let this discourage you from building your platform. IT-savvy firms experiment on the platform—to generate value through reuse. And they also experiment off the platform—to identify the next breakthrough idea. You can—indeed, you must—do both.

TAKE THE LEAD ON DRIVING VALUE

One constant in the efforts of IT-savvy firms to drive value from IT is the leadership of senior business executives. Here are things you need to do to drive strategic value from IT:

- *Set the direction:* Define an operating model that establishes the parameters for your digitized platform. Articulate the strategic vision that the operating model, and underlying platform, is intended to realize.

- *Lead the transformation:* Direct major initiatives to build a digitized platform. Take responsibility for the organizational changes needed to execute the vision.

- *Preserve technology, data, and process standards:* Provide oversight of the operating model and the platform enabling it. Require that technology implementations conform to the standards or justify the exception.

- *Drive the value:* Take advantage of the business agility your digitized platforms offers. In response to new market opportunities, (1) encourage empowered employees to continuously improve your firm's business processes; (2) innovate constantly on your platform; (3) reorganize, as necessary, to maximize customer responsiveness; and (4) install the platform—and the accompanying organization changes—in appropriate acquisitions. And don't forget to experiment off the platform.

Is it worth your time and effort to lead your firm on the IT savvy journey? Absolutely! If senior executives do not lead the effort to become IT savvy, their firms will never get there. The digitized platform will not materialize, and IT will fulfill only isolated promises.

Certainly, you have too many other duties to take sole responsibility for driving value from your digitized platform. In addition to the senior management responsibilities listed earlier, you need to find a way to engage everyone in the firm in driving value from IT. This takes us back to governance. So, build a platform. Govern it effectively. Then let everyone in your firm drive success. The opportunities are boundless.

7

Leading an IT-Savvy Firm

By now we hope you're convinced that you should become IT savvy and build a digitized process platform for your firm. Being IT savvy pays off. Our research found that firms that are above average on both IT savvy and IT spending have margins 20 percent higher than industry average. In contrast, firms with less than average spending and savvy have margins 32 percent lower than their industry.[1] Just as important, being IT savvy puts you in a position to take advantage of future business opportunities.

In this chapter, we ask you to first assess your firm's IT savvy. Then we discuss the leadership roles necessary to lead you through the IT savvy journey. We also discuss what vendors can do to help you become savvier. We close with a Monday morning mandate—what you and your colleagues should do next. Unless you take the lead and change behavior, you won't become IT savvy, and IT will be more of a liability than an asset.

HOW IT SAVVY IS YOUR FIRM?

Our research has identified five sets of practices and competencies that characterize IT-savvy firms. Consider your firm's practices in each of these five areas, and then we will ask you to self-assess your IT savvy.

- *How committed are you and your senior management colleagues to using IT strategically?* Driving value from IT requires senior management attention and commitment. This means you need to communicate—over and over—the firm's operating model to set the direction. Then you need to attend and actively participate in committee meetings addressing IT issues. It's also your job to establish criteria for IT funding and to monitor outcomes of IT projects. Remember, commitment is not just a matter of saying IT is important. In a recent assessment of IT savvy for a financial services firm, top managers rated themselves highly on their IT commitment. But customer-facing people and other executives in that firm scored top management commitment much lower. The different results surprised and disappointed the senior executive team. One senior manager asked "How come they don't get it?" Actions matter. If senior managers aren't constantly demonstrating commitment to using IT strategically, there isn't enough commitment.

- *How well are you integrating business and IT?* In IT-savvy firms every person thinks digitally. Your goal is to have a single source of truth from your key data; digitized process components for your core business processes; and a limited set of standard technologies. In the same way that every business plan has a budget, the business plans of IT-savvy firms contain a section on the role of technology. Every business strategy considers the implications for IT, and the IT unit plays a role in envisioning what strategies are possible. You'll want regular briefings about technology trends and their implications for your industry, with case studies of competitors and interesting practices. One sign that you've achieved IT-business integration is general acceptance of the CIO as a business leader.

- *How well do you manage politics?* IT is inherently an integrating technology. IT integrates processes within the firm and integrates the firm with its customers and suppliers. Anything that inhibits that integration reduces the effectiveness of the firm's IT spending. Firms whose people are reluctant to share data and business processes and that don't have a culture of collaboration and sharing have lower IT savvy. One of our favorite examples comes from our study of the valve manufacturing industry. The sales group was excited about introducing high-end laptops for salespeople.

Customers were very impressed when the salesperson in the customer's office could design and then schedule their custom order online and guarantee a delivery date. When the firm first implemented the system, however, the production manager was resistant and announced "no flaky salesperson is going to touch my production schedule." The in-customer-office order entry system outlasted the production manager. Politics is a powerful force and often much more subtle and subversive than the reaction of a particular production manager. Becoming IT savvy requires building a shared sense of community supported by the right mix of local and global incentives. Without that sense of community, dysfunctional politics undermine enterprise IT initiatives.

- *How empowered are your people with great systems and information?* The bottom line of being IT savvy is that the users of the systems are able to do their jobs effectively and feel empowered to excel. Before Delta Airlines built its digitized platform, if you asked "What gate is flight 56 departing from?" you could get a different answer from the curb-side check-in agent, the telephone service agent, and the Crown Club room service agents. Each person was looking at different systems and getting a different answer. Not only were customers frustrated, but so were Delta agents, who wanted to do a great job.[2] Satisfaction with IT systems, IT services, and data is fairly easy to measure. Many firms, including Intel, Novartis, Procter & Gamble, and JM Family, measure employee satisfaction with the quality of their IT services regularly, some benchmarking with a cohort of similar firms. Some firms include external customer satisfaction too. Make these satisfaction measures transparent in your firm and typically they will improve over time. Empowering your people with great systems is part of being IT savvy.

- *How well do you learn from experience?* IT-savvy firms learn from experience and don't make the same mistakes over and over. For example, we know intuitively that we shouldn't spend any money on IT before we optimize the business process. We know this, we really do—but somehow in the heat of the moment we don't always do it. IT-savvy firms embed their lessons from the past—and from other firms—into their governance processes. Practically, these lessons come to life as gates in the project methodology to ensure that the mistakes of the past aren't repeated. Rather than be perceived as obstacles, these gates add value by enabling reuse, sharing, and faster time to market. There is a learning curve, however, and initially there will be resistance. Widely disseminated testimonials of great successes, the right balance of local and global incentives, transparency of decision processes, and a quick exception process all help your firm learn from experience.

Like the firms in this book, you will become IT savvy and build a digitized platform gradually—one project at a time.

You'll have to refine your IT governance processes to incorporate new learning. Simplify and discard mechanisms that don't work and reinforce a culture of learning from experience.

BENCHMARK YOUR FIRM'S IT SAVVY

In the appendix we have provided a questionnaire that will allow you to assess your firm's IT savvy. The results from many firms we've benchmarked in the past make up a bell-shaped curve, and you'll be able to see where you fit on that curve. Please take about ten minutes now to answer those questions. Then read the explanation in the appendix about how to interpret your score and what your score says about the actions you should take.

One other way to assess how IT savvy your firm has become is to do the following calculation for each major IT project:

$$\text{ROI}_{\text{business case}} - \text{ROI}_{\text{post-implemtation review}}$$

Total the results for all of last year's major projects. In IT-savvy firms, this total approaches zero. As you become more IT savvy, you get better at estimating benefits and delivering on those estimated benefits. Because typically only IT-savvy firms do post-implementation reviews, just being able to calculate this measure is evidence of IT savvy!

KEY ROLES IN IT-SAVVY FIRMS

Chapter 1 identified three obsessions of IT savvy firms: fix what's broken, build a digitized platform, and exploit the platform for profitable growth. All of senior management, not just the CIO, needs to be obsessive about these tasks. The IT savvy journey offers opportunities and challenges for everyone in the firm. Table 7-1 summarizes the key IT leadership roles. We review three of those roles here.

You and Every Senior Executive

You and your senior colleagues are a critical success factor in your firm's IT savvy journey. It is up to you and your colleagues to build an IT-savvy culture and define the operating model. Then allocate the resources to implement the model, determine the level of commitment, communicate and encourage desirable behavior, and assess progress. No one else in the firm has the clout to do this.

Because building and using a digitized platform is a process of changing your firm to adapt to the demands of the digital economy, you will either tackle these responsibilities or your firm will continue to find IT an obstacle to—rather than an enabler of—business success. Once you make the commitment to build a digitized platform, you will find that, to get on board, the rest of your people need clear performance metrics and transparency regarding decision processes.

Given all these expectations for the senior management team, you may be wondering what we've left for the CIO. The answer is: plenty. The CIO is part of the senior management team and thus shares in all the responsibilities described earlier. But the CIO also has a unique role to play—arguably the most important role in the firm for making a firm IT savvy.

TABLE 7-1

Key IT leadership roles

CEO and senior business executives	• Clarify the operating model and what will be standard and shared. • Reinforce standards for business process, data, and technology. • Budget for off-platform innovation. • Fund and resource major initiatives to build the platform. • Determine IT funding priorities and oversee performance. • Build a digital culture and assign accountabilities for digitized platforms and firmwide business processes. • Design governance and incentives reinforcing desirable behavior.
CIO and senior IT leaders	• Run world-class IT operations, making performance transparent and adding services over time. • Manage enterprise data to empower employees. • Develop technology standards and compliance and exception processes to build your platforms. • Ensure buy-in to project methodology, business cases, and post-implementation reviews. • Develop IT unit costing process and pricing of shared IT services. • Champion services and processes to be shared and standardized.
Strategy execution officer (SEO or process owners)	• Design the business process and data requirements for the digitized platform. • Manage change and implementation—including optimizing processes, systems, and training. • Design performance metrics and the organizational changes required.
Business unit leaders	• Clarify local operating model and innovate on the platform. • Buy into or challenge enterprisewide operating model. • Develop local system requirements. • Develop business cases. • Track business value against business cases.
Project leaders	• Implement project methodology. • Make first-level exception decisions. • Do post-implementation reviews.

Source: © 2009 MIT Sloan Center for Information Systems Research. Used with permission.

The Role of the CIO

The CIO is responsible for the smooth running of 24 × 7 IT operations, IT governance, and implementation of new projects. The CIO also has a unique vantage point and is one of the few executives who sees across the entire firm. Thus, the CIO is well positioned to recognize what can be standardized and shared across the firm.

Table 7-1 highlights some of the key responsibilities of the CIO for running IT operations and working with business leaders to define enterprise business process and data standards. But many CIOs tell us that their role is changing. Beyond managing their enterprise's IT organization, some CIOs own business processes, others have revenue targets, others manage a network of IT outsourcers, and still others manage shared services including HR, financial services, and sourcing.

CIOs allocate time in four major areas. To better understand the job of the CIO and help you determine what kind of CIO you need, we studied how CIOs allocate their time. We found that CIOs allocate their time into four major roles and that most CIOs allocate some time to each. In the parentheses are the average time allocations for each role.[3]

- *Managing IT services (44 percent of CIO time):*
  Managing the IT organization and its people and vendors to ensure delivery of IT infrastructure, applications, and related services across the company at the desired cost, risk, and service levels

- *Working with non-IT colleagues (36 percent):* Working with non-IT colleagues, both enterprisewide and within business units, addressing issues such as business strategy, business process optimization, new product or service development, acquisitions, regulatory compliance and risk, and IT investment prioritization

- *Working with customers (10 percent):* Meeting with the company's external customers, partners, and colleagues as part of the sales or service delivery process, including establishing electronic linkages with customers

- *Managing enterprise processes (10 percent):* Managing enterprise processes and the associated digitized platform, including shared services, product development, global supply chain, customer experience, operations, corporate responsibility, and green issues

Although the average CIO spends 44 percent of his or her time managing IT services, these average time allocations mask a lot of individual variation. For example, Richard Hoynes, Tyco's CIO during 2007–2008, inherited a company coming out of significant turmoil. His focus was on delivering world-class IT services at the lowest possible unit cost. To achieve that goal, Hoynes spent more than 50 percent of his time on the IT services tasks, particularly project delivery and IT planning, with a focus on measuring results such as IT unit cost and project delivery.

In contrast, Patricia Hewlett, former CIO and vice president of IT at ExxonMobil, delegated most of the responsibilities for running IT day to day to one of several very capable direct reports. She allocated 75 percent of her time to working with non-IT executives on business strategy, innovation, acquisitions, major projects, and IT spending prioritization.

Rosalee Hermans, CIO of Timberland, a US$1.7 billion apparel and footwear firm, has a solid IT infrastructure. She spends 15 percent of her time "making Timberland easy and inexpensive to do business with" and "having automated conversations with customers," with a particular focus on developing the growing small to medium-sized market in Asia and elsewhere.

We have classified CIOs into four types—services, embedded, external customer, and enterprise processes—based on how they spend their time. Each type of CIO spends above-average time in one of the four roles. Table 7-2 describes these four types.

As firms increase their IT savvy, the responsibilities of the CIO will evolve. We believe all CIOs will still allocate time to all four roles but that the emphasis will change as IT savvy increases. In stages 1 and 2 of the journey (see chapter 4) the CIO must focus on the services CIO role. Continued breakdowns or poor IT service are unsustainable for any CIO. The CIO in stage 2 of the IT savvy journey needs to be a tough-minded person with C-suite support who moves the firm relentlessly toward technology standardization.

Once the services CIO role has been mastered, the CIO can focus on the embedded role working on business process and data issues and on ensuring effective IT governance of the firm. As the firm becomes comfortable with established governance,

TABLE 7-2

Four types of CIOs

	Services	Embedded	External customer	Enterprise processes
% of current CIO searches	50% 1↓[a]	30%↑	10%↑	10%↑
Focus	IT services at right quality and cost	Work with non-IT colleagues; strategy, business process execution, and innovation	Help sell and deliver the firm's services and make the firm easy to do business with	Manage enterprise processes (e.g., operations, product development, shared services)
CIO activity with above-average time allocation	Manage IT services (above 44% of CIO time)	Work with non-IT colleagues (above 36% of CIO time)	Work with customers (above 10% of CIO time)	Manage enterprise processes (above 10% of CIO time)
Key metrics	• IT unit cost and service levels • Internal consumer satisfaction • Budget and people management	• Business agility • Peer review • Firmwide financial performance	• Revenue targets • Customer service costs • External customer satisfaction	• Business process performance or measures concerning special projects

Source: © 2009 MIT Sloan Center for Information Systems Research. Used with permission.

a. Based on 2009 estimations of the demand for hiring of CIOs by Shawn Banerji, managing director of Russell Reynolds. Arrows represent direction of trends.

the CIO will become more focused on either the enterprise processes or the customer CIO role. The customer CIO role will likely emerge in firms where the CIO can play a major part in the sales or delivery process (e.g., technology and services vendors, some financial services, telcos). In other firms, we see the CIO moving toward enterprise process management and perhaps a new role—the strategy execution officer, or SEO.

The Role of the SEO

We have been discussing how IT-savvy firms build and use digitized platforms. However, few firms have identified a single executive-level owner of the core business process platform. As a result, at many firms, the potential benefits of the platform have not materialized.[4]

Enter the SEO—the strategy execution officer. Although no one we know has this title, it is our generic name for a role that has emerged in some top-performing firms. The SEO takes ownership of the enterprise's core business processes. In some firms, the CIO has taken on this role. In other firms, the role is filled by the COO, the senior vice president for global supply chain, the head of shared services, or a more general executive vice president.

Everyone with an SEO type of role has three major responsibilities for building and driving value from the digitized platform:

1. *Build the digitized platform:* The first responsibility of an SEO is to plot the changes in technology, business processes, and data required to build the digitized platform. The entire senior management team must define the high-level vision and decide what will be shared across the enterprise. But firms need a single leader to

lead the effort and decide what to do, when. The SEO accepts accountability for defining priorities in the development effort.

2. *Lead the change:* The organizational change required to implement standard business processes is painful. The entire senior management team must embrace change, but massive change requires a point person. The SEO fills that role, ensuring ongoing training on new processes and systems. The SEO at some firms has taken on general responsibility for process discipline and continuous improvement, such as six sigma efforts.

3. *Drive value from the platform:* Getting systems in place is only the initial challenge facing an SEO. The ongoing challenge is to generate benefits from the platform. The SEO is responsible for measuring the performance of a core process to ensure that the firm achieves required behavior changes and their expected outcomes. To clarify management expectations, the SEO, often with other senior executives, may need to change incentives, organizational structures, or both.

At BT, CIO Al-Noor Ramji took on the role of CIO and head of the customer experience. At Dow Chemical Company, CIO Dave Kepler heads global supply chain and shared services. Filipo Passerini at Procter & Gamble runs Global Business Services. These are all SEO roles at firms that recognized they could not benefit from a digitized platform unless they put a strong leader in charge. If you have a technology platform that isn't creating expected business benefits, think about appointing an SEO.

Table 7-1 outlines some IT leadership roles deeper into the organization as well. The IT savvy journey starts with senior executives, the CIO, and, at some firms, the SEO. But business and IT leaders throughout the enterprise also play key roles. It's important to define those roles and hold managers accountable.

THE ROLE OF VENDORS AND PARTNERS

We've outlined the roles of key people inside the firm, but there is also a huge industry of IT service providers and business process outsourcers available to help you become more IT savvy. In fact, the potential for outsourcing both technology management and business processes may diminish your commitment to embarking on the IT savvy journey. Don't let that happen. You should, however, view the IT services industry as a partner on your journey.

The Role of Vendors in Small and New Firms

The widespread availability of high-quality external IT and business process services means that most new firms need not develop deep expertise in technology management. If you are a leader in a small or relatively young firm, you can rely on a strong IT partner to provide the necessary technical expertise and manage your firm's IT requirements as it grows. As the firm evolves, you'll be able to choose which processes to perform internally and which to perform externally. A good vendor partner can contribute ideas, upgrade technology, and apply effective technology management practices. Many vendors can even help you shape a digitized platform and then run the technology and the business processes for you.

But remember that your digitized platform is the foundation for your business. Regardless of how much help you get, you must own the operating model, the design, the business rules, and the business initiatives you drive from it. All of the problems that plague long-established firms remain risks for newer firms—with or without vendor partners. With so many vendors to choose from, it's easy to get into the habit of chasing down the next great offer from the next persuasive salesperson. But that habit will almost certainly lead you down the path of using IT for tactical rather than strategic goals.

The design of—and commitment to—a digitized platform is senior management's responsibility. No vendor can spare you from bad decisions. And no vendor can drive value from IT for you. You can take a partner on the IT savvy journey *with* you, but you can't ask that partner to take the journey *for* you.

The Role of Vendors in Large, Global Firms

More-established and larger firms should also take advantage of the IT services market. Campbell Soup has effectively used a vendor partner to help it first clean up its IT operations and then take over most responsibility for running operations, but this has involved an intensive management effort on the part of both client and vendor.[5] Together they worked to undo bad habits in Campbell's management and use of IT. What this means for you is that IT vendor partners can help you on your IT savvy journey, but they don't let you skip any stages.

Dow Chemical Company started calling on vendors for help building a digitized platform in the early 1990s.[6] One of Dow's partners provides project management and development support; another runs infrastructure operations. With the help of these partners, Dow has built a digitized platform supporting a global supply chain, a highly standardized manufacturing environment, and all of the firm's shared administrative services. The platform has helped Dow maintain profitability in a commodity industry.

Going forward, Dow's senior management team expects the firm's success to depend more on the development and sale of specialty chemicals, and Dow has been relying heavily on joint ventures to do the product development. Over 25 percent of Dow's revenue is generated from joint ventures. Dow's digitized platform, however, was not built to meet the unique requirements of joint ventures. To update the firm's digitized platform, management's preference is to find a set of vendor partners who can update and run key transaction systems as well as perform many basic business processes and services.

We've noted that once a digitized platform is built, a firm must constantly refresh it. This constant tweaking can be disruptive throughout the firm (think about the last time your firm upgraded your desktop software). Dow's idea is to outsource its digitized platform as large components to specialist firms and let them worry about the refreshing. So far, Dow has found interested vendors but no real market. Thus, at this point, modular outsourcing of the digitized platform of a large global firm appears to be challenging, risky, and expensive.

We do anticipate that as more firms build digitized platforms, the market for the kind of services Dow is seeking will materialize. Even very large firms will have the option of sending many technology and base-level business processes to firms specializing in these services. But don't think that means you can wait to become more IT savvy. The firms best positioned to take advantage of these kinds of services will be those who are well along on the IT savvy journey.

IT-savvy firms understand their digitized business processes—and the components of those processes—well enough to recognize which can be handled by a services provider and which ones they need to keep in-house. And the systems and processes constituting their platforms are designed in such a way (i.e., not like cold spaghetti) that components can be extracted from the rest of the platform. So don't expect a vendor to make you IT savvy. But start working with vendors who can enhance your technology services and help you build your platform.

THE IT SAVVY MONDAY MORNING MANDATE

Becoming more IT savvy is everyone's responsibility. We hope that for readers who have made it this far, the benefits are clear and compelling and we have mapped out the journey with some clear signposts. We trust we have provided a number of motivating examples of firms that have achieved greatness in part due to their IT savvy.

Now it is up to you to make your firm more IT savvy every year. It is up to you and your senior management colleagues to build the digitized platform that will enable your profitable growth in the digital economy. We leave you with a set of seven actions you can take today to start making your firm more IT savvy. Think of these seven actions as your IT savvy Monday morning mandate:

1. *Debate your operating model:* IT cannot do anything strategic for you until you decide how you want to operate. Remember that IT does two things well—standardizing and integrating. Make the most of what IT can do.

2. *Design your IT governance on one page:* Based on your strategic priorities, determine the small set of governance mechanisms that will engage all stakeholders in working to achieve your goals.

3. *Clarify your expectations of—and performance metrics for—your CIO (and perhaps SEO):* This exercise should engage you and the CIO/SEO in an honest discussion of the role of IT, its current strengths and weaknesses, and the stage of the IT savvy journey that your firm is in.

4. *Create a transparent IT funding and prioritization process:* State the criteria and specify who will make decisions and be accountable.

5. *Put someone (very capable) in charge of designing and executing a post-implementation review process:* Start learning now from your current projects.

6. *Assess your IT savvy (see appendix):* Make a plan for addressing the major problem areas.

7. *Help your people become more IT savvy:* Making all your people more IT savvy is a firmwide effort and a great role for HR, perhaps in partnership with IT. Work with the HR director to ask: How effective is our professional development related to IT savvy? How empowered are our people by our systems? How is this measured?

A digitized platform allows you to continuously optimize and pull costs out of your core processes. At the same time, it provides a foundation for both innovation and agility for your people to exploit. Over time, the new offerings become part of an ever-richer platform—and the virtuous cycle of innovation and standardization continues. The results are profitable growth and empowered people. We wish you well on your IT savvy journey and urge you to take the lead.

How IT Savvy Are You and Your Colleagues?

Please consider the part of the firm you know best when answering the questions in the following assessment.[1] There are five categories of questions, each with a box for your answer. For the first category—"Top Management Commitment to Information Technology"—please read through the statements, considering your firm. Then choose an answer from plus 8 (strongly agree—e.g., walk-on-water good) to minus 8 (strongly disagree—e.g., drowning) that best represents your firm's effectiveness at all the practices and competencies listed. If you think your firm is about average for your industry, please enter a zero. Then repeat the process for the other four categories.

1. Top Management Commitment to Information Technology

Senior Managers:	−8	0	+8

- Attend IT council meetings themselves and don't send a nominee. _____ (handwritten: +)

- Define the target degree of business process standardization and integration and the necessary capabilities of the digitized platform (e.g., business processes, data, and technology). _____ (handwritten: −2)

- Require carefully considered business cases for investments with measures and responsibilities identified. _____ (handwritten: −4)

- Support the strategic uses of IT by providing seed funding not requiring traditional net present value financial justifications and stopping poorly performing projects early. _____ (handwritten: −8)

- Encourage post-implementation reviews that are not witch-hunts, and facilitate the gathering and dissemination of the lessons learned. _____ (handwritten: −8)

- Encourage, fund, and actively support training in the use of IT. _____ (handwritten: −4)

2. Integrating IT with Business

In your firm there are/is:	−8	0	+8

- Executive management considerations of information and IT implications in business strategy discussions. _____ (handwritten: ✓)

- Regular high-level briefings on the implication of IT developments in your industry. _____ (handwritten: ✓)

- Accountabilities for achieving strategies that are clear and documented. _____

- Articulation of the respective roles and responsibilities of business and IT management in achieving effective and efficient systems and delivering business benefits. Managers are named and held accountable. _____

3. Organizational Politics and Political Turbulence

Your firm:	−8	0	+8

- Exhibits a strong sense of community, a feeling of shared interests and purpose and cooperation among managers. This is reinforced with reward systems and incentives that are based on the right balance of firmwide and local measures. _____

- Captures relevant data in one business area and willingly shares it across the firm. Cross-functional and business opportunities are actively sought to innovate, improve service, and reduce costs. _____

- Encourages cooperation via cross-functional teams, secondments, and movement of personnel. _____

---

4. Empowered and Satisfied Users

There is:	−8 0 +8
• A feeling of empowerment for all people in the firm resulting from immediate access to data and systems that helps with their jobs.	_____
• Confidence in the reliability of systems and the completeness of information.	_____
• A sense of relevance and accuracy of the information in the systems.	_____
• Excellent support provided to those using the systems. Help desks are very effective, and assistance from technical personnel is excellent.	_____
• Excellent user understanding resulting from easy-to-use systems and good training.	_____
• The attitude and responsiveness of those who provide support for systems is enthusiastic and professional.	_____

5. Learning from Experience

Your firm always:	−8 0 +8
• Redesigns, simplifies, or reengineers business processes before any money is spent on information systems.	_____
• Maximizes the reuse of business process and information systems components.	_____
• Ensures that every new IT project that is not infrastructure has a businessperson as champion with clearly identified deliverables and responsibilities of the business and IT people.	_____
• Ensures that infrastructure investments are treated separately from investments in applications to take account of their shared nature and long life.	_____
• Encourages innovative use of IT in the business units even if firmwide standards are not always followed. Integration can be achieved later if successful.	_____

INTERPRETATION

Now add up the five scores to get a total ranging from minus 40 to plus 40. The more colleagues from your firm who complete this self-assessment, the more accurate the results. Then just average the results for all the respondents. It's also interesting to look at the differences in average scores from different parts of the firm (e.g., IT and non-IT, home country and non–home country, large and small business units, customer facing and back office). Based on our statistical analysis of hundreds of firms, your score is a rough approximation of the percent premium your firm gets from its IT investments relative to the average. The IT savvy scores of many firms make up a bell-shaped curve with top and bottom scores of plus 40 and minus 40 (figure A-1). Thus, if your firm has an IT savvy score of plus 6, you earn about a 6 percent premium

FIGURE A-1

Bell-shaped curve of IT savvy scores

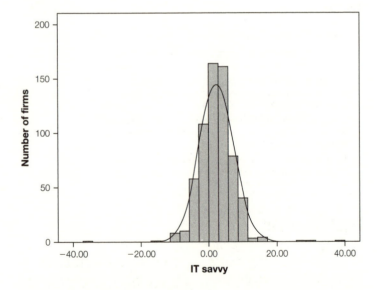

Source: © 2009 MIT Sloan Center for Information Systems Research. Used with permission.
Mean = 2.3; standard deviation = 5.1; sample of 640 firms from 23 countries.

on each dollar you invest in IT relative to the average firm. If your score is minus 9, you get a return of about 9 percent below the average.

So what does your score suggest you should do? If your IT savvy score is:

- *Above plus 20:* First take a moment to celebrate—and then ask why. If the answer is a firmwide understanding of digitization and mature IT governance processes that is part of your culture, then take more business risk with IT. Spend more on IT than your competitors and reweight your IT portfolio to the more risky asset classes such as revenue-generating uses of IT (i.e., strategic) and enterprisewide infrastructure. Being savvier will mitigate the inherent riskiness of those investments. If the high IT savvy scores are the result of the talents of a few individuals, it's time to convert those individual efforts into your governance processes and eventually the culture. Otherwise, when those individuals move on to other roles, IT savvy will slip backward.

- *Between 0 and plus 19:* The return you get per dollar invested in IT is above the industry average, but there are still areas ripe for improvement. Take a look at the five categories of IT savvy questions in the assessment. Then choose the one or two categories in which you had the lowest scores. Look down the list and think about the items that made you give a lower score. Pick one, and make it your personal target to improve your and your colleagues' performance on those items—and talk about it. The result will be greater IT savvy and higher returns per dollar invested in IT.

- *Between minus 1 and minus 19:* The return you get per dollar invested in IT is below the industry average, and there are a number of areas for improvement. Follow the same process as in the previous paragraph, but realize that the urgency is greater. You are leaking more value per dollar invested in IT than the average firm and it's time to increase IT savvy—make it a project and someone's responsibility. If your score is below minus 9, we suggest you consider deferring some IT projects, particularly the more risky revenue-generating and infrastructure projects, until IT savvy is increased.

- *Between minus 20 and minus 40:* Your case for action is urgent because the leakage of value is severe. We recommend a temporary measure to have all IT projects approved by the CEO or CFO to ensure tougher controls until IT savvy is increased. Focus on projects with ROIs based on clear cost savings, and defer large infrastructure projects where possible. A task force should be formed to improve the IT savvy of the organization. If one business unit is savvier than another, consider transferring personnel and practices to the less savvy unit.

With attention, IT savvy will increase over time. Using this same questionnaire, you can assess IT savvy every year and compare different parts of the firm.

NOTES

Preface and Acknowledgments

1. Niccolò Machiavelli, *The Prince,* trans. R. M. Adams (New York: Norton, 1977), 1513.

Chapter 1

1. The material on Aetna in this chapter is primarily drawn from Cyrus F. Gibson, "Turnaround at Aetna: The IT Factor," working paper 362, MIT Sloan School of Management Center for Information Systems Research, Cambridge, MA, 2006.

2. From a presentation entitled "Leading Change: A Conversation with Ron Williams" made as part of the MIT Sloan School of Management's Dean's Innovative Leader Series on October 9, 2008 (http://mitworld.mit.edu/video/614).

3. Enterprise resource planning systems (often referred to as ERPs) are a way to integrate the data and processes of an organization into a single system. Customer relationship management systems (or CRMs) are focused on customer information and optimizing customer relationships. The two major providers of ERP and CRM software are SAP and Oracle, although many smaller firms serve medium and small companies.

4. For further details on how 7-Eleven Japan uses IT for strategic advantage, please see Kei Nagayama and Peter Weill, "7-Eleven Japan Co., Ltd.: Reinventing the Retail Business Model," working

paper 338, MIT Sloan School of Management Center for Information Systems Research, Cambridge, MA, 2004. Also see 7-Eleven Japan's Web site, http://www.sej.co.jp/english/.

5. See Jeanne W. Ross, "United Parcel Services: Delivering Packages and E-Commerce Solutions," working paper 318, MIT Sloan School of Management Center for Information Systems Research, Cambridge, MA, 2001, for a description of UPS's development of an IT capability.

6. For further details on P&G's shared services organization, see Peter Weill, Christina Soh, and Sia Siew Kien, "Governance of Global Shared Solutions at Procter & Gamble," research briefing vol. VII, no. 3A, MIT Sloan School of Management Center for Information Systems Research, Cambridge, MA, 2007.

7. MIT Sloan CISR survey of 1,508 firms in sixty countries in late 2007, in which the CIO and IT finance person (in the same firm) were surveyed. See Peter Weill, Stephanie L. Woerner, and Howard A. Rubin, "Managing the IT Portfolio (Update Circa 2008): It's All About What's New," research briefing vol. VIII, no. 2B, MIT Sloan School of Management Center for Information Systems Research, Cambridge, MA, 2008.

8. For more information about the benefits of a digitized platform, see Jeanne W. Ross and Peter Weill, "Understanding the Benefits of Enterprise Architecture," research briefing vol. V, no. 2B, MIT Sloan School of Management Center for Information Systems Research, Cambridge, MA, 2005.

9. "How Good Is Your Online Nurse?" *Businessweek Online*, February 20, 2006, http://www.businessweek.com/magazine/content/06_08/b3972117.htm.

10. For further details on this research, see Peter Weill and Sinan Aral, "Generating Premium Returns on Your IT Investments," *Sloan Management Review* 47, no. 2 (2006): 39; and Peter Weill, Stephanie Woerner, Sinan Aral, and Anne Johnson, "Becoming More IT Savvy and Why It Matters," research briefing vol. VII, no. 1D, MIT Sloan School of Management Center for Information Systems Research, Cambridge, MA, 2007.

Chapter 2

1. This section draws on Rebecca Chung, Donald Marchand, and William Kettinger, "The CEMEX Way: The Right Balance Between Local Business Flexibility and Global Standardization," Case IMD-3-1341 (Lausanne, Switzerland: IMD, 2005). See also Cemex Corporation's 2007 annual report: http://www.cemex.com/CEMEX_AR2007/ENG/default.html.

2. Jeanne W. Ross, "United Parcel Services: Delivering Packages and E-Commerce Solutions," working paper 318, MIT Sloan School of Management Center for Information Systems Research, Cambridge, MA, 2001.

3. Mike Eskew former CEO of UPS, MIT Sloan School of Management Center for Information Systems Research video interview, April 16, 2002.

4. This section draws on Peter Weill, Christina Soh, and Sia Siew Kien, "Governance of Global Shared Solutions at Procter & Gamble," research briefing vol. VII, no. 3A, MIT Sloan School of Management Center for Information Systems Research, Cambridge, MA, 2007.

5. This section draws on interviews conducted by Jeanne W. Ross and Cynthia M. Beath with executives at PepsiAmericas in May 2008. Used with permission.

6. This section draws on David C. Robertson, "ING Direct: The IT Challenge (B)," working paper IMD-3-1345, IMD, Lausanne, Switzerland, 2003.

7. "ING DIRECT Growing, Kuhlmann Says," *News Journal* (Wilmington, DE), October 21, 2008.

8. For more details on ING DIRECT's governance processes, see Peter Weill and Jeanne W. Ross, *IT Governance: How Top Performers Manage IT Decision Rights for Superior Results* (Boston: Harvard Business School Press, 2004), 161–162.

9. This section draws on Cynthia M. Beath and Jeanne W. Ross, "Information and Transformation at Swiss Re: Maximizing Economic Value," working paper 373, MIT Sloan School of Management Center for Information Systems Research, Cambridge, MA, 2007.

10. Yury Zaytsev and Jeanne W. Ross, "Building a Global Operating Platform at Swiss Reinsurance Company," research briefing vol. VIII, no. 1B, MIT Sloan School of Management Center for Information Systems Research, Cambridge, MA, 2008.

11. Beath and Ross, "Information and Transformation at Swiss Re."

12. Adapted from Jeanne W. Ross, Peter Weill, and David Robertson, *Enterprise Architecture as Strategy: Creating a Foundation for Business Execution* (Boston, Harvard Business School Press, 2006).

13. Beath and Ross, "Information and Transformation at Swiss Re."

14. For more information on Pfizer's organization, see Weill and Ross, *IT Governance*, 172–173.

15. Assumptions about Federal Express's operating model are based on author reading of publicly available information. See for example: Ali F. Farhoomand and Pauline Ng, "FedEx Corp.: Structural Transformation Through e-Business, Harvard Business School Case #HKU098, January 1, 2000, revised August 1, 2007.

16. The measure for strategic implementation effectiveness was a weighted average of the company's priorities for operational efficiency, customer intimacy, product leadership, and strategic agility relative to its success in meeting each objective.

17. Based on a survey of 103 companies. These were perceptual measures of how well the company's existing IT-enabled business processes were addressing each of these strategic needs. The first three strategic impacts refer to the disciplines described in Michael Treacy and Fred Wiersema, *The Discipline of Market Leaders: Choose Your Customers, Narrow Your Focus, Dominate Your Market* (Reading, MA: Addison-Wesley, 1995). We added strategic agility because of its growing importance to companies.

18. Operating models of subunits will be bound by their unit's operating model. This means that the operating model of a subunit (e.g., business unit) must be at least as integrated or standardized as the unit's (e.g., firm's) operating model. Thus, a subunit's operating

models should be the same as the unit's model or to the right or up on the 2 × 2 matrix shown in figure 2-1.

Chapter 3

1. The material on BT is drawn from Nils O. Fonstad, "Strengthening Engagement to Achieve IT-Enabled Transformation," BT Case Study: Part B, in preparation; Nils O. Fonstad, "Enhancing Engagement at BT: An Update," research briefing vol. VII, no. 1B, MIT Sloan School of Management Center for Information Systems Research, Cambridge, MA, 2007; and "CIO 100 2008 Winner Profile: BT Group," *CIO Magazine*, http://www.cio.com/cio100/detail/1811.

2. Jeanne W. Ross and Cynthia M. Beath, "Building Business Agility at Southwest Airlines," working paper 369, MIT Sloan School of Management Center for Information Systems Research, Cambridge, MA, 2007.

3. From an MIT Sloan School of Management Center for Information Systems Research (CISR) survey of 1,508 firms in sixty countries conducted late in 2007. This number is the percentage of firms who answered that their post-implementation reviews were 4 or 5 on a scale from 1 (not effective) to 5 (highly effective).

4. MIT Sloan CISR 2007 survey (see note 3).

5. Ibid.

6. For more information see Peter Weill, Stephanie L. Woerner, and Howard A. Rubin, "Managing the IT Portfolio (Update Circa 2008): It's All About What's New," research briefing vol. VIII, no. 2B, MIT Sloan School of Management Center for Information Systems Research, Cambridge, MA, 2008.

7. This section is based on a stream of work on IT portfolio management at the MIT Sloan School of Management Center for Information Systems Research and the Melbourne Business School and draws on the following sources: Peter Weill and Sinan Aral, "Generating Premium Returns on Your IT Investment," *MIT Sloan Management Review* 47, no. 2 (2006): 39; and Sinan Aral and Peter Weill, "IT Assets, Organizational Capabilities, and Firm Performance: How Resource Allocations and Organizational

Differences Explain Performance Variation," *Organization Science* 18, no. 5 (2007): 763.

8. Mark Jeffery and Igmar Leliveld, "Best Practices in IT Portfolio Management," *MIT Sloan Management Review* 45, no. 3 (2004): 41. The study with interviews of 130 *Fortune* 1000 firms' CIOs in 2003 was conducted by Diamond, International and the Kellogg School of Management. The measure of profit was return on assets.

9. The EMC case study is based on a series of interviews with senior IT and non-IT EMC executives by MIT Sloan CISR researchers Peter Weill and Stephanie Woerner in 2007 and Jeanne Ross in 2008.

10. Percentages are based on a 2007 MIT CISR survey of 157 firms in the same industry.

Chapter 4

1. Material for the discussion of Swiss Re is drawn from Yury Zaytsev and Jeanne W. Ross, "Building a Global Operating Platform at Swiss Reinsurance Company," research briefing vol. VIII, no. 1B, MIT Sloan School of Management Center for Information Systems Research, Cambridge, MA, 2008.

2. See the Swiss Re Web site, http://www.swissre.com.

3. These stages were previously reported in Jeanne W. Ross, "Creating a Strategic IT Architecture Competency: Learning in Stages," *MIS Quarterly Executive* 2, no.1 (2003): 31; also see Jeanne W. Ross, Peter Weill, and David C. Robertson, *Enterprise Architecture as Strategy: Creating a Foundation for Business Execution* (Boston: Harvard Business School Press, 2006).

4. All the statistics in this chapter (unless noted) are from the MIT Center for Information Systems Research survey in late 2007 of 1,508 firms in sixty countries.

5. Quoted from Rebecca Rhoads, "Leading the IT Organization at Raytheon" (presentation at the MIT Sloan School of Management Center for Information Systems Research Summer Session, June 2005).

6. Jeanne W. Ross and Cynthia M. Beath, "Building Business Agility at Southwest Airlines," working paper 369, MIT Sloan School of Management Center for Information Systems Research, Cambridge, MA, 2007.

7. Tom Steinert-Threlkeld, "Nestlé Pieces It Together," *Baseline* 54 (2006): 36.

8. Given the small sample size and high costs of early adoption, the high IT operating budgets may overstate the spending patterns of firms that move to stage 4 in the future.

9. Material for the discussion of eBay is drawn from a presentation of CIO Brad Peterson at MIT Sloan School's class 15.571 "Getting Business Value from IT" and a videotaped interview at MIT CISR of Brad Peterson on 13 March 2008. Further information is from www.ebay.com.

10. Steven C. Wheelwright, Charles A. Holloway, Christian G. Kasper, Nicole Tempest, Cisco Systems, Inc.: Acquisition Integration for Manufacturing (A), Harvard Business School Case #600015, August 10, 1999, revised February 15, 2000.

11. "Amazon Web Services," http://aws.amazon.com/.

12. Interviews conducted by Jeanne W. Ross and Cynthia M. Beath with executives at PepsiAmericas in May 2008. Used with permission.

Chapter 5

1. Mike Eskew, former CEO of UPS, MIT Sloan School of Management Center for Information Systems Research video interview, April 16, 2002.

2. See Peter Weill and Jeanne W. Ross, *IT Governance: How Top Performers Manage IT Decision Rights for Superior Results* (Boston: Harvard Business School Press, 2004), 14. This result is from 116 for-profit firms listed on U.S. exchanges. Assessed by the CIO, governance effectiveness was the firm's success in delivering four IT objectives weighted by importance: cost-effective use of IT, and effective use of IT for asset utilization, revenue growth, and business flexibility. Governance effectiveness has statistically significant positive relationship with several measures of financial performance (i.e., return on equity, market cap growth).

3. The Campbell case study is drawn from Jeanne W. Ross and Cynthia M. Beath, "Campbell Soup Company: Harmonizing Processes and Empowering Workers," working paper 374, MIT Sloan School of

Management Center for Information Systems Research, Cambridge, MA, 2008.

4. Firms without these five mechanisms have statistically significantly lower IT governance effectiveness (see note 2 for details).

5. The sources for the State Street Corporation case study are: Peter Weill and Richard Woodham, "State Street Corporation: Evolving IT Governance," working paper 327, MIT Sloan School of Management Center for Information Systems Research, Cambridge, 2002; Peter Weill and Jeanne W. Ross, *IT Governance: How Top Performers Manage IT Decision Rights for Superior Results* (Boston: Harvard Business School Press, 2004); and interviews with State Street executives in 2002, 2003, 2004, 2005, 2006, 2007, and 2008; and http://statestreet.com/.

6. Figure 5-3 was developed by Peter Weill and Nils O. Fonstad from the IT engagement model framework developed by Nils O. Fonstad. For more information on the IT engagement model, see Nils O. Fonstad, "Enhancing Engagement at BT: An Update," research briefing vol. VII, no. 1B, MIT Sloan School of Management Center for Information Systems Research, Cambridge, MA, 2007.

7. See Weill and Ross, *IT Governance*, 13, where the result was 38 percent. In our subsequent MIT Sloan School of Management Center for Information Systems Research surveys in 2005, 2006, 2007, and 2008, the result gradually improved to 46 percent.

8. See Weill and Ross, *IT Governance*, 218.

9. Jeanne W. Ross, Peter Weill, and David Robertson, *Enterprise Architecture as Strategy: Creating a Foundation for Business Execution* (Boston: Harvard Business School Press, 2006); and Rebecca Rhoads, CIO Raytheon Corporation (presentation during MIT Sloan School of Management Center for Information Systems Research Summer Session, Cambridge, MA, June 16, 2005).

Chapter 6

1. Details on 7-Eleven Japan are drawn from Kei Nagayama and Peter Weill, "7-Eleven Japan Co., Ltd.: Reinventing the Retail Business Model," working paper 338, MIT Sloan Center for Information

Systems Research, Cambridge, MA, 2004; Ben M. Bensaou, H. Uchino, K. Mitani, and M. Noishiki, "7-Eleven Japan: Managing a Networked Organization," 05/7-4690, INSEAD Euro-Asia Centre, 1997; and visits from MIT CISR researchers.

2. 7-Eleven Japan's history of innovations is from http://www.sej.co.jp/english/company/history.html.

3. This list of initiatives related to business agility resulted from interviews of thirty-two IT executives conducted by Jeanne W. Ross and Cynthia M. Beath in the fall of 2005. See Jeanne W. Ross and Cynthia M. Beath, "Enabling Agility: People, Process, and Technology," research briefing vol. VI, no. 1C, MIT Sloan School of Management Center for Information Systems Research, Cambridge, MA, 2006.

4. Jeanne W. Ross and Cynthia M. Beath, "Campbell Soup Company: Harmonizing Processes and Empowering Workers," working paper 374, MIT Sloan School of Management Center for Information Systems Research, Cambridge, MA, 2008.

5. The Sarbanes-Oxley Act of 2002 created a five-member public company accounting oversight board, which has the authority to set and enforce auditing, attestation, quality control, and ethics standards for auditors of public companies. (From AICPA, "Landmark Accounting Reform Legislation Signed into Law," http://www.aicpa.org/pubs/cpaltr/Sept2002/landmark.htm.)

6. Cynthia M. Beath and Jeanne W. Ross, "Information and Transformation at Swiss Re: Maximizing Economic Value," working paper 373, MIT Sloan School of Management Center for Information Systems Research, Cambridge, MA, 2007.

7. Peter Weill, Christina Soh, and Sia Siew Kien, "Governance of Global Shared Solutions at Procter & Gamble," research briefing vol. VII, no. 3A, MIT Sloan School of Management Center for Information Systems Research, Cambridge, MA, 2007.

8. David C. Robertson, "ING Direct: The IT Challenge (B)," working paper IMD-3-1345, IMD, Lausanne, Switzerland, 2003; and Peter Weill and Jeanne W. Ross, *IT Governance: How Top Performers Manage IT Decision Rights for Superior Results* (Boston: Harvard Business School Press, 2004), 161–162.

9. Jeanne W. Ross, "United Parcel Services: Delivering Packages and E-Commerce Solutions," working paper 318, MIT Sloan School of Management Center for Information Systems Research, Cambridge, MA, 2001.

10. The discussion of PepsiAmericas' customer segmentation draws on interviews conducted by Jeanne W. Ross and Cynthia M. Beath with executives at PepsiAmericas in May, 2008. Used with permission.

11. Cynthia M. Beath and Jeanne W. Ross, "Information and Transformation at Swiss Re: Maximizing Economic Value," working paper 373, MIT Sloan School of Management Center for Information Systems Research, Cambridge, MA, 2007.

12. The discussion of CEMEX is based on Rebecca Chung, Donald Marchand, and William Kettinger, "The CEMEX Way: The Right Balance Between Local Business Flexibility and Global Standardization," Case IMD-3-1341 (Laussanne, Switzerland: IMD, 2005); and Rebecca Chung, Katarina Paddack, and Donald Marchand, "CEMEX: Global Growth Through Superior Information Capabilities," Case IMD-3-0953 (Laussanne, Switzerland: IMD, 2003).

13. For an explanation of the dangers of disruptive technological change, see Clayton Christensen and Michael Overdorf, "Meeting the Challenge of Disruptive Change," *Harvard Business Review*, 1 March 2000, Reprint R00202.

14. See http://dell.com for more information on Dell's business model and product and services line.

15. Jeanne W. Ross, "United Parcel Services: Delivering Packages and E-Commerce Solutions," working paper 318, MIT Sloan School of Management Center for Information Systems Research, Cambridge, 2001 for a description of UPS' development of an IT capability.

Chapter 7

1. Peter Weill and Stephanie Woerner, "Becoming More IT Savvy: And Why It Matters," research briefing, vol. VII, no. 1D, MIT Sloan School of Management Center for Information Systems Research, Cambridge, MA, March 2007.

2. Jeanne W. Ross, "E-Business at Delta Airlines: Extracting Value from a Multi-Faceted Approach," working paper 317, MIT Sloan School of Management Center for Information Systems Research, Cambridge, MA, 2001.

3. This section on the CIO is derived from: Peter Weill and Stephanie L. Woerner, "How CIOs Allocate Their Time," research briefing vol. VIII, no. 1A, MIT Sloan School of Management Center for Information Systems Research, Cambridge, MA, 2008; and Peter Weill and Stephanie L. Woerner, "The Future of the CIO," research briefing vol. IX, no. 1, MIT Sloan School of Management Center for Information Systems Research, Cambridge, MA, 2009.

4. Jeanne W. Ross and Peter Weill, "Who Owns Strategy Execution in Your Company?" research briefing vol. VII, no. 2C, MIT Sloan School of Management Center for Information Systems Research, Cambridge, MA, 2007; and Jeanne W. Ross and Peter Weill, "All Roads Lead to the SEO," *The Wall Street Journal*, June 16, 2007.

5. For more information on Campbell's outsourcing arrangements, see chapter 7 in Jeanne W. Ross, Peter Weill, and David Robertson, *Enterprise Architecture as Strategy: Creating a Foundation for Business Execution* (Boston: Harvard Business School Press, 2004), 143. We encourage firms considering IT and business process outsourcing to read this chapter to better understand how outsourcing relates to building a digitized platform.

6. For more information on Dow's outsourcing initiatives, see Jeanne W. Ross and Cynthia M. Beath, "The Federated Broker Model at The Dow Chemical Company: Blending World Class Internal and External Capabilities," working paper 355, MIT Sloan School of Management Center for Information Systems Research, Cambridge, MA, 2005.

Appendix

1. For more than ten years, the MIT Sloan Center for Information Systems Research has collected data on IT investments, IT-savvy practices and competencies (measured in several different ways), and firm performance (relative to industry competitors). Firms that had

effectively implemented the practices and competencies described in the twenty-five items in the assessment presented in this appendix also had statistically significantly higher financial performance impacts from their IT investments. The questions in the assessment are representative of the practices and competencies exhibited by IT-savvy firms but don't cover the full set. For more information, see Peter Weill and Sinan Aral, "Generating Premium Returns on Your IT Investment," *MIT Sloan Management Review* 47, no. 2 (2006): 39; Sinan Aral and Peter Weill, "IT Assets, Organizational Capabilities, and Firm Performance: How Resource Allocations and Organizational Differences Explain Performance Variation," *Organization Science* 18, no. 5 (2007): 763; and Peter Weill, Stephanie Woerner, Sinan Aral, and Anne Johnson, "Becoming More IT Savvy and Why It Matters," research briefing vol. VII, no. 1D, MIT Sloan School of Management Center for Information Systems Research, Cambridge, MA, 2007.

INDEX

Peter Weill is Chairman of the MIT Sloan School of Management's Center for Information Systems Research (CISR) and an MIT Senior Research Scientist. His research and advisory work centers on the strategic impact, value, and governance of IT in enterprises. He has presented widely at industry forums, executive education classes, and MBA programs on the business value of IT and has published award-winning books, journal articles, and case studies. These include his books with Jeanne W. Ross, *Enterprise Architecture as Strategy: Creating a Foundation for Business Execution* (also with David C. Robertson) and *IT Governance: How Top Performers Manage IT Decision Rights for Superior Results* (Harvard Business School Press, 2004). He also coauthored the bestseller *Leveraging the New Infrastructure: How Market Leaders Capitalize on Information Technology* (Harvard Business School Press, 1998) and *Place to Space: Migrating to eBusiness Models* (Harvard Business School Press, 2001), which won one of the Library Journal of America's best business book of the year awards. In 2008

Ziff-Davis recognized Peter as number 24 of the "Top 100 Most Influential People in IT."

Jeanne W. Ross is Director and Principal Research Scientist at the MIT Sloan School of Management's Center for Information Systems Research. Her research centers on the organizational and performance implications of enterprise initiatives related to enterprise architecture, governance, and new IT management practices. At MIT she lectures, conducts research, and teaches public and customized executive courses on IT management. She has published widely, including journal articles, book chapters, and case studies. Her prior books, coauthored with Peter Weill, *Enterprise Architecture as Strategy: Creating a Foundation for Business Execution* (also with David C. Robertson) and *IT Governance: How Top Performing Companies Manage IT Decision Rights for Superior Results*, were also published by Harvard Business School Press. She regularly speaks at major forums discussing IT management and value, and she is a founding senior editor and editor-in-chief of *MIS Quarterly Executive*.